CW00550461

# Thatch, Towers and Colonnades

*The story of architecture in Southport*

by Cedric Greenwood

*Carnegie Publishing*
1 9 9 0

*To all those who welcomed me into their homes*
*They made this book possible*

*Thatch, Towers and Colonnades*
by Cedric Greenwood

First published, 1971 by *The Southport Visiter*, Southport.
This edition extenisvely revised and expanded, 1990

Published by Carnegie Publishing Ltd.,
18 Maynard Street, Ashton, Preston PR2 2AL
Designed and typeset in Times, Caslon, Plantin and Bodoni Openface by Carnegie Publishing Ltd.,
Printed and bound by H. Charlesworth & Co. Ltd., Huddersfield

Copyright, © Cedric Greenwood, 1971 and 1990

**All rights reserved**
No part of this publication may be reproduced, stored in a retrieval system or transmitted in any form or by any means mechanical, electronic, photocopying, recording or otherwise, without the prior permission of the publisher.

**ISBN 0 948789 64 6**

# *Contents*

# *Foreword*

*by the late Colonel Roger Fleetwood Hesketh*
*former Lord of the Manor of North Meols*

WHEN Victoria ascended the throne we entered an era known to architectural historians as the 'battle of the styles', a battle which has continued to the present day. Nowhere can the progress of this conflict be better observed than in the streets of Southport.

With the large-scale urban developments of the eighteenth century, the lessor maintained a rigid control not only of the layout but also of the elevations. We observe the successful results of this policy at such places as Bath and Buxton, as well as in London's Belgravia. Urban landowners of the nineteenth century, while retaining control of the layout, did not usually attempt to secure uniformity of elevation. The fact that terrace building tended to go out of fashion may have been a contributory cause of this change of policy but I believe that the main underlying reason lay in the fact that the lessees, unlike those of the eighteenth century, who accepted the prevailing style as a matter of course, were unwilling, with so many styles to choose from, to accept the straitjacket of a particular idiom which did not accord with their personal tastes. Southport is a good example of this type of development. While the lessors provided a harmonious setting, the lessees, with the wealth of Liverpool and Manchester behind them, were able to indulge their fancies without having to count the cost too closely.

One regrets that this book was not written some years ago, for we have recently lost a number of buildings of architectural merit. For example, the charming late-Georgian villas, which had to make way for the two tall blocks of flats which now face the roundabout at the east end of Lord Street, the Victoria Hotel, which gave the Promenade its special character, and the Pier Pavilion which, with others of its kind, must surely have been a direct descendant of the Prince Regent's Pavilion at Brighton.

But in a town like this the task of the preservationist is not easy. When redevelopment becomes necessary it is sometimes possible to preserve long, uniform and unbroken façades while adapting the building behind to conform to modern requirements, as has been done so successfully with the Regent's Park terraces and the Rue de Rivoli in Paris. But where the buildings are detached and in different styles it is seldom possible to resist the economic forces generated by the increase in site values and changes in public demand which have occurred since the house was built.

Until well into the present century all the land upon which Southport is built was contained within the boundaries of three private estates. It was always possible for one of these, if only as an act of enlightened self-interest, to forego an immediate profit in order to preserve or enhance the amenities of the town. But these estates have now disintegrated and, while the listing of buildings by the Department of the Environment has done something to protect works of outstanding architectural merit, it is exceedingly difficult for a public authority, especially in borderline cases, to impose sanctions on someone who has bought in the open market a particular site for a particular purpose. But if one cannot always save an old building there is every reason for seeking to replace it with something equally good and for that reason I agree with the author when he advocates an extension of the planning authority's control of the appearance of new buildings.

Mr Greenwood is to be congratulated not only for making us aware of the merits of many buildings that we have been gazing at all our lives with unseeing eyes but also for having provided a record which will be welcomed by students of architecture far beyond the confines of this town.

*R. F. Hesketh*
Meols Hall
November, 1971

# *Preface*

THE wise man built his house upon a rock, the foolish man built his house upon the sand but the men who built Southport on a desolate stretch of coastal sandhills transformed a waste into a beautiful town.

The first lords of the manor of embryonic Southport were Peter Hesketh Fleetwood of Rossall Hall near Fleetwood and Henry Bold Houghton of Bold Hall near Warrington. They laid out Lords' Street (as it was called then) 88 yards wide between the building lines. The width of the street was determined by nature, the houses being built along both sides of a wide hollow, which was swampy in the wet season, between the parallel ranges of dunes. The contemporary Lancashire historian, Edward Baines, said they were 'handsome red-brick houses with large gardens in front.'

Lord Street was the first boulevard in the world. The wide, straight street lined with trees and gardens predates the boulevards of Paris, Boston, Philadelphia and Washington. Prince Louis Napoleon rented a house in Lord Street for a few months in 1838 before he became Emperor Napoleon III of France and directed the layout of the Paris boulevards, which in turn inspired those in America.

The Lord Street gardens were laid out by the Improvement Commissioners from the 1860s, using the long front gardens of the houses along the inland side of the street and the present gardens were laid out in the 1920s and '30s to a very much modified plan of 1911 by the eminent landscape architect, Thomas Mawson of Lancaster.

The town has grown up as the home and place of retirement of wealthy Liverpool and Manchester businessmen and thus has a very high standard of building and architecture. There is a surprising wealth of architecture in Southport hidden away behind the trees if you know where to look for it. Essentially Victorian, Southport was built in an age of individualism and is a rich kaleidoscope of architectural styles.

This book is intended as a guide to the buildings worth looking at and describes them against a sketched-in background of the history of Southport and the history of architecture. It is intended to encourage a public awareness and interest in the built environment to safeguard and improve our amenities.

Architecture is an art and of all the arts it must be the most satisfying. It is three-dimensional, executed on a large scale and is seen, used and experienced by the general public. An awareness and understanding of architecture not only makes us feel at one with our town but makes travel very much more interesting and deepens our appreciation of every city, town and village we visit.

This book began as a series of articles I wrote in the *Southport Visiter* from January 1969, to April 1971. They were reconstructed, revised and rewritten with many additional buildings and photographs in the first edition of this book published by the *Visiter* in 1971. That, in turn, has been updated and extensively rewritten with further additional buildings and new photographs for this second edition published by Carnegie Publishing of Preston. Original photographs have been used where the buildings have not been altered, even though the names on the fascias might have changed, or, in some cases, to show how the buildings looked before they were altered.

My thanks to all the owners and tenants of the buildings featured for allowing me to look around and feature their property, to the staff of the Atkinson Reference Library and innumerable other sources of information and to the *Southport Visiter* for the use of some of the original collection of photographs taken by the late Joe Sadler, the late George Latham and the late Tom Ball.

*Cedric Greenwood*
Campbeltown
Argyllshire
October, 1990.

Chapter One

# *Thatched Cottages*

IT might surprise many Southport visitors and even residents—and certainly those who have never been here—to know that this modern Lancashire seaside resort has thirty thatched homes nestling among the straight lines of red brick and slate.

There are twenty in Churchtown, five in Marshside, four in Southport proper and one in Birkdale. All but one are cottages built between 1600 and 1720. The odd ones out are a large house at 46 Beach Priory Gardens, which was built in 1936 with a thatched roof, and a thatched bungalow built as an extension at the back of the old thatched cottage at 54 Shellfield Road in 1989.

There used to be many more thatched cottages standing among the sandhills now covered by the town of Southport. Birkdale in 1900 had thirty-three cottages—twenty-two thatched and eleven slated.

Most of the cottages in the old parish of North Meols have disappeared in the development of modern Southport but there are still many to be seen standing on odd corners, huddled together in rows or hidden away behind the street frontage—little oases of the past, incongruous in their urban setting.

Some of them back onto the road and you have to 'go round the back' into the 'front' garden to call at the door. Then you notice that all the old cottages in Marshside and most of the others in the town face in the same direction—between south and south-east. They were built this way—before roads were of any significance—so that the gardens, porches and main windows catch the sun.

Some of the older cottages, like many an old barn in south-west Lancashire, were built by the mediaeval 'cruck' form of construction, which was still used in remote areas long after the Middle Ages. The crucks were pairs of bent tree trunks or long, curving beams, leaning together and jointed at the apex in arches the shape of whale jawbones (or chicken wishbones). They stood on large slabs of stone as foundations. Tie beams, rafters, purlins and collar beams, all joined by wooden pegs, completed the framework and the walls were made of wattle-and-daub, which in this area consisted of clay reinforced with straw, star grass from the dunes, horsehair—and layers of whitewash.

All the cottages were originally thatched because it was cheaper to

*This long thatched cottage at 1 Botanic Road, Churchtown, has been home to the same family for five generations. The vaulted ceiling of the parlour shows roof timbers that are evidently from an old sailing ship. The cottage was a farmhouse for 240 years and the old shippons and stables are still at the back. [photo,* Southport Visiter*]*

*Numbers 2, 4 and 6 Botanic Road—three Hesketh estate cottages in Churchtown. [photo,* Southport Visiter*]*

*One of the majority of old Southport cottages that has exchanged its thatched roof for a slate one. No 83 Roe Lane still makes a charming picture of an old English country cottage. It has more charm than the two thatched cottages next door, which have been spoilt with the phoney S-shaped timbering. [photo, Cedric Greenwood]*

*Rustic Southport: the cottage at the end of Cockle Dick's Lane has been home to Gil Blundell for 44 years and to his ancestors since before 1845. [photo, Cedric Greenwood]*

thatch a roof in the grain growing areas of south-west Lancashire and the Wirral than to bring stone or slate from the uplands. Today some cottages retain their old mud partition walls but all outer walls are brick and most roofs have been slated because a slate roof, although more expensive to put on, is much cheaper to maintain. Thatch always wants patching up and a complete rethatch is needed every twenty to thirty years and costs anything from £2,000 to £5,000 a time, depending on the size of the roof. Most thatches are now covered with plastic netting to keep the birds out.

While most cottages have lofts or false ceilings, a few, like 1 Botanic Road and 74 Liverpool Road, retain the vaulted roof space over the parlour, showing the crucks and roof timbers. Some of the purlins and rafters have a slight curvature together with notches and bolt holes that seem to have no purpose in the construction. Many of the roof timbers of Southport cottages are said to be ships' timbers from wreckage washed up on the shore. The cottages stood much closer to the receding sea in the seventeenth and eighteenth centuries than they do today and the shore provided a ready source of building materials.

Just as in the depths of the countryside, many of the thatched cottages in Southport have been the birthplace of successive generations of the same families that live in them today. None of the present occupants of any of the thirty thatched houses in Southport would swap their thatched roof for a slate one. They all say the houses are warm in winter and cool in summer because the thatch is good insulation.

The Hesketh estates, which own eighteen of the twenty thatched cottages in Churchtown say that, despite the cost of thatching and the difficulty of getting long straw in these days of combine harvesting, their policy is and always will be to maintain the outward appearance of their cottages while modernising them inside.

Developers, however, are less altruistic. Despite today's trend to

*Thorntree Cottage, 43 Coudray Road, Southport, a rustic touch in suburbia.*
*[photo, Cedric Greenwood]*

*Rus-in-urbe, Sally's Lane, Churchtown.*
*[photo, Cedric Greenwood]*

conservation, restoration and building new thatched houses, Southport has lost four unlisted thatched cottages in the eighteen years since the first edition of this book. Those at 17 Halsall Road and 48 Mallee Crescent have been demolished for new houses, while the pair at 8 and 10 Threlfall's Lane burned down to be replaced by a new bungalow.

We would have lost 74 Liverpool Road to redevelopment as well had it not been spot-listed as a result of local representations.

The charming thatched cottage at 54 Shellfield Road has been extended at the back to four times the size of the original. It is now a thatched bungalow and gone, gone is the enchanting cottage garden that was the setting for the opening of this chapter in the first edition—along with the clip-clop of the shrimper's cart. It has been replaced by an equally enchanting oasis of rus-in-urbe in the garden created by the new owners of what is known officially as 38 St. Cuthbert's Road but is approached by Sally's Lane.

Southport enters the 1990s and maybe even the twenty-first century still with thirty thatched homes. Here is a complete list of them:

Churchtown: 1, 11, 13, 50, 52, 54, 54A and 96 Botanic Road; 2, 4, 6 and 12 Back Botanic Road; 187 and 189 Cambridge Road; 9 Churchgate; 2 Moss Lane; 22, 36, 38 and 40 St. Cuthbert's Road.

Marshside: 24 Knob Hall Lane; 123, 125 and 127 Marshside Road; 54 Shellfield Road.

Southport: Cockle Dick's Lane; 46 Beach Priory Gardens; 79 and 81 Roe Lane.

Birkdale: 74 Liverpool Road.

Besides its thatched cottages, Southport has many other cottages that were once thatched. The one at 83 Roe Lane is more picturesque than the two thatched cottages next door at 79 and 81. These two cottages were converted from a farmhouse and have been spoilt with phoney timbering for decorative effect; S-shaped timbers would not help support a timber frame.

Thorntree Cottage, 43 Coudray Road, is another rustic touch in suburbia. The purlins are made from a ship's mast split down the middle. The groups of cottages at Chase Heys in Beresford Drive and Bank Nook in Radnor Drive are also worth seeing. Those at Chase Heys are particularly small with low doors; the roofs are much deeper than the walls and they were obviously once thatched.

*St. Cuthbert's presides over a group of thatched cottages in Cambridge Road, Churchtown. [photo, Cedric Greenwood]*

Chapter Two

# *Meols Hall*

VIEWED across the open country from the east, against the backdrop of trees, Meols Hall presents a serene picture of an eighteenth-century country house behind a wide lawn framed by two classical gazebos—a scene ostensibly unchanged over two hundred years.

On the west side of the hall, behind the trees, is the former village of Churchtown, now a busy suburb of Southport. The hall is also illusory; the present building dates from the mid-seventeenth century but its appearance today is largely the creation of the 1960s. The most pleasing architectural features of Meols Hall are the work of the last lord of the manor, the late Colonel Roger Fleetwood Hesketh (1902 to 1987), and built in the period 1960-64. Like an architect who stepped out of the eighteenth century, Colonel Hesketh, self-taught in the three-dimensional art, drew detailed plans, made models, hired the craftsmen individually and supervised the work.

When he took over the hall in 1938 it was a relatively nondescript pitched-roof house. The older and larger part of the hall had been pulled down in 1733. The Colonel extended and transformed the house not in the grand manner of the eighteenth century but in a much more pleasing and interesting non-symmetrical composition of tastefully modest classicism, retaining the gabled bay of 1695. The result is a house that looks as if it has grown organically over the years, with a varied roofline and a three-dimensional frontage on both its east and west aspects.

The rebuilding of Meols Hall was done not so much as an architectural exercise as to house the large collection of family paintings and other works of art from the former family home at Rossall Hall on the Fylde coast.

The Colonel designed the reconstruction from the inside out: the size of the paintings and his designs for their display dictated the size of the rooms and the internal arrangement dictated the external plan.

Meols Hall is the last home of the Hesketh family, whose estates once covered most of the coastal area from Southport to Heysham. There has been a manor house on this site since the early thirteenth century, when the manor was granted to Robert de Coudray, of

*The east front of Meols Hall, showing, from the left, the south wing, the 1695 gable and the mid-17th-century main block. [photo, Cedric Greenwood]*

Penwortham. It has remained in the possession of his family and descendants to the present day, passing by marriage into the Hesketh family, of Rufford, at the end of the sixteenth century.

When the Hesketh were linked by marriage with the Fleetwoods of Rossall Hall on the Fylde coast in 1733 they pulled down a large part of Meols Hall and moved home to Rossall. For a hundred years Meols Hall was tenanted by agents and in 1835 it became a farmhouse.

The Hesketh lived at Rossall until 1844, when Sir Peter Hesketh Fleetwood had to sell his Fylde coast estates to pay for the new town of Fleetwood. His younger brother, Charles Hesketh, had become rector of North Meols in 1835 and so the old rectory in Roe Lane (then Row Lane) became his home. After his death in 1876 his widow built a new rectory and renamed the old one The Rookery, where the family continued to live.

Meols Hall was used as a military hospital in World War One and in 1919 the Hesketh returned to the hall after an absence of 186 years. The extensions of the 1960s restored the hall to something like its original size.

Before inheriting the family seat, Roger Hesketh was owner of the *Master Builder* magazine, the official organ of the National Federation of House Builders, from 1933 to 1937. It was a joint venture with his brother, the late Peter Fleetwood Hesketh, of Hale, who later became national secretary of the Victorian Society and author of 'Murray's Lancashire Architectural Guide.'

'Peter and I thought we might be able to convert builders' taste,' he said. 'I wrote articles and Peter did the drawings for the houses we hoped they would build instead of what they were already doing.' Roger promoted his belief that the best modern architecture could be achieved by a return to classical principles, proportion and restraint.

When Roger moved into Meols Hall in 1938, he was not to know that he had to wait another twenty-two years before he could put his principles into practice. He was an officer in the intelligence service during the 1939-45 war. After the war he was held up by building

restrictions. He was High Sheriff of Lancashire in 1947, Mayor of Southport in 1959 and MP for Southport from 1952 to 1959. Then his opportunity came.

The Colonel did not enter into any contracts, nor did he employ a clerk of works. He engaged bricksetters, stonemasons, slaters, joiners, plumbers and plasterers, paid for their time and materials and supervised them himself. This not only cut costs but gave greater flexibility to adapt the design to practical considerations as the work progressed.

Nearly all the bricks used in these works, together with the slates on the central block, came from Tulketh Hall, near Preston, which once belonged to the Hesketh family and was demolished in 1959, the year before work started at Meols Hall. The quoins and rusticated door surrounds on the east front and on the gazebos came from Lathom House, near Ormskirk, when its north wing was pulled down in 1960. Other stone dressings, including the cornice, were made of concrete using ground Lathom stone in the mixture and cast on site in home-made moulds.

In the rebuilding of Meols Hall, the mid-seventeenth century main block had the east front remodelled with projecting bays each side of the central garden room to house extensions of the dining room and drawing room. A cornice and an attic storey were added and the whole front was faced in old brick and stone from Tulketh Hall and Lathom House.

On the west front of the main block, the first- and second-floor windows were deepened and the pitched roof was fronted by a cornice and a brick parapet with small pediments that echo the original gables.

The Colonel added a late-Georgian style two-storey south wing with some dummy windows to break up what would otherwise be plain walls, the attractive bow-fronted single-storey north wing, housing the library, and the rusticated stone and brick gazebos with battlements at the north-east and south-east corners of the garden.

The gazebos are modelled on the one at Rossall, the last vestige of that old hall, standing on the sea bank, but the Meols Hall gazebos have rusticated doors and Georgian windows instead of the brick niches of the early-eighteenth-century gazebo at Rossall.

Colonel Hesketh's late-Georgian interiors are particularly pleasing; the curved-in walls to the doorway at the inner end of the entrance hall, the semi-elliptical archways in the corridors and the oval skylight shaft that tapers upwards over the main stairway.

The main block houses the entrance hall, the dining room, the yellow room (a sitting room), the study and the garden hall on the ground floor, bedrooms and bathrooms on the first floor and the box-room and study on the second floor.

The oval skylight over the main stairway pierces an old 'priest hole', a hiding place for Roman Catholic priests who lodged at the hall during the purges of the Reformation. Lancashire has always been a strong Roman Catholic county and the Hesketh were members of the Roman Church until the middle of the eighteenth century.

Adjoining the central block on the south, the 1695 gable houses the gun-room and the pantry-and-china room on the ground floor and bedrooms and bathrooms on the upper floors.

*The drawing room built in the 1960s. It houses some of the family's art collection. In the centre is a large Berlin china urn with landscape paintings of Charlottenburg and Sans Souci. By the west wall stands an early-18th-century Chinese lacquer cabinet.*
*[photo,* Southport Visiter.*]*

*The Yellow Room contains beams similar to those at Rufford Old Hall and Carr House, Bretherton, of the same period. Against the north wall is a mid-18th-century Chinese lacquer cabinet.*
*[photo,* Southport Visiter.*]*

*A lifesize painting of Sir Peter Hesketh Fleetwood's Arab stallion by James Ward in 1828 determined the height of the south wall in the library from the dado rail to the cornice.*
*[photo,* Southport Visiter.*]*

*The Palladian-style shippon at Meols Hall.*
*[photo, Cedric Greenwood]*

The ruined dovecot on the lawn and the great barn in the farmyard are contemporary with the mid-seventeenth century central block and built of the same two and a half inch brick as the west front.

*The west front of Meols Hall, showing, from left to right, the single-storey north wing housing the library (1960-4), the three-bay main block (mid-17th-century), the 1695 gable and the two-storey south wing (1960-4).*
*[photo,* Southport Visiter.*]*

The old barn has mullioned windows in its north wall. Colonel Hesketh added a Palladian-style shippon to the farm buil-dings, with colonnades and a semi-elliptical fanlight over the main door. In the true tradition of the eighteenth century the colonel's architectural detail extended right down to the cowshed.

The shippon was, in fact, one of his first buildings, dated 1951. He actually made a start on alterations at Meols Hall in 1938, when he built a small single-storey library extension at the north end of the west front but this was considerably enlarged in the 1960s.

The present art collection at Meols Hall includes portraits by Cornelius Jansen, Hogarth, Arthur Devis, Wright of Derby, Romney, Raeburn and Sir Thomas Lawrence, landscapes by Jan Breughel, Gaspard Poussin, Michau, Tillemans, Paul Sandby and Morland, a life-size painting of an Arab stallion by James Ward, plus silverware, china and Renaissance furniture. In the entrance hall are three carved oak chairs, which were in Westminster Abbey at Charles II's coronation.

*A gazebo at Meols Hall.*
*[photo, Cedric Greenwood]*

o OOO o

Chapter Three

# *Regency and Gothick*

THE town of Southport had its birth in a group of 'marine residences' built among the sandhills in a place called 'over the Nile' . . . later Nile Square . . . now Lord Street West. The Nile is a brook which drains Halsall Moss to the sea along the south side of the line of Duke Street. It now runs in culvert. It was named after Nelson's victory at the battle of the Nile in 1798, the same year as Southport's birth. Both heroes of the Napoloenic wars, Nelson and Wellington, are commemorated in the names of adjacent streets and terraces, built early in the nineteenth century.

Dr. Miles Barton (1725 to 1810), who lived at Much Hoole and practised at Ormskirk, advocated sea bathing at North Meols for health and sent many invalids here. He is credited with naming the locality South Port and the brook the Nile. The naming ceremony took place at the housewarming party at William Sutton's hotel—at what is now the south end of Lord Street—in 1798 and he named the hostelry the South Port Hotel.

Until then, the site of modern Southport was known as South Hawes—the (sand) hills on the south bank of the Ribble estuary. The new suffix Port was given because of a deep-water anchorage offshore, the South Channel of the Ribble estuary, where ships anchored awaiting the tide to go into Preston.

A creek called Fairclough's Lake ran inshore at North Meols (Churchtown), used by the local fishing fleet and small coasters loading and unloading. There was a customs house at North Meols in the latter part of the seventeenth century and for most of the eighteenth century. The creek silted up towards the end of the eighteenth century but the name South Port was established and adopted to distinguish the growing new town of villas by the Nile from the fishermen's cottages and shanties among the South Hawes.

In the Victorian period, Southport looked like a port, with its three quarter mile pier, its fishing fleet of more than a hundred smacks, the ships and tugs at anchor waiting to go into Preston and the paddle steamers at the pier head on excursions to Blackpool, Llandudno and Douglas. The South Channel silted up from the 1880s with the extension of the Ribble main channel revetment walls, the accumulation of

*The Willows, 2 Lord Street West, is the most beautiful and attractive of the remaining 'marine residences' of embryonic Southport, built around 1800.*

dredgings from the Mersey, the diversion of Crossens Channel from South Channel to Pinfold Channel and land reclamation between Southport and Hesketh Bank.

To return to the 1790s, Bland's *Annals of Southport* (1867 to 1902) record that in 1797 'Mr Bold Fleetwood Hesketh was appointed High Sheriff, an event which led to the foundation of the town of Southport.

'Meols Hall, being much more convenient of access to the various Lancashire towns than Rossall, the former became the Sheriff's principal headquarters, at which the county families were entertained. 'As a result a number of the gentry took leases of land near the coast and erected marine residences', says Bland.

They were brick villas, most faced in stucco, with white painted paling enclosing gardens, many of which featured figure-heads and other relics from wrecked ships, washed up on the shore.

*This extension to The Willows was built in 1924, a perfect match to the old house.*

A Mrs Moneypenny is named by Bland as one of the ten 'first residents of Southport' in 1798. She lived in Willow Cottage, which was later extended and renamed Willow Grove.

Today it is The Willows, 2 Lord Street West, withdrawn behind the trees and lawns of its long front garden, the most beautiful and attractive of the remaining 'marine residences' of early Southport.

Standing at the head of a long, curving driveway up a gently graded sweep of lawn and guarded by two ornamental globular lamps, the long, low, two-storey house presents a wide panorama of stuccoed late-Georgian architecture: broad and bold in outline with a Classical pediment and

Gothic details.

Antiquarians introduced Gothic details into Georgian towards the end of the eighteenth century to add a certain picturesque quaintness and called it 'Gothick'. These details are seen here in the late-Gothic or Tudor arch windows, their rectangular, stepped hood mouldings or dripstones, and the battlements on the porch. The black rusticated quoins, or cornerstones, which are characteristic Georgian, match the battlements on the porch and along the garden wall.

The interesting thing is that the south end of the house—over that embattled garden wall—with the Tuscan pillars in the porch, was built in 1924 and completely matches the style of the house that was built more than 125 years before to make it one homogeneous edifice.

Although Lord Street West describes a graceful curve, notice how the houses along it are built in straight, parallel lines, wide apart—the lines of the former Nile Square.

It is hard to imagine that, although today Lord Street West is part of the A565 main road axis along which the linear town is built, it was once a secluded square, partitioned off by the South Port Hotel, which stood across the south end of Lord Street. The hotel was pulled down in 1854 to open up a link between Lord Street and the new development of Birkdale Park, and Nile Square was renamed Lord Street West.

From its embryo around the mouth of the Nile, Southport grew north along and around the valley in the sandhills that is now Lord Street. By 1850 it was a small town (population 4,200) stretching from Nile Square to the lower end of Manchester Road and consisting mainly of two-storey Regency villas and terraces with modest Grecian and Italianate hotels along the Promenade, all finished in stucco with painted wooden shutters—a small oasis of Mediterranean classical refinement in a desert of sand on the edge of the sea.

Regency architecture was the last phase of Georgian and the point in architectural history where the Italian Renaissance and the Greek Revival converged. Columns and pilasters were more often of the original Greek orders. Regency was Gothic as well as classical and many of Southport's Regency houses have quaint, narrow Tudor arch windows and other 'Gothick' features, executed with characteristic Regency delicacy.

Southport has now grown into a town of 90,000 people in a built-up area extending seven and a half miles along the coast from Crossens to Woodvale and up to two miles inland at Kew.

Few towns of this size still have private houses on the main street but one of the attractive features of Lord Street is that among the shopping colonnades, banks, offices, supermarkets, hotels, luxury apartment towers, gardens, fountains and monuments nestle small groups of two-storey homes dating from the early nineteenth century, when Lord Street was, for the most part, a street of private residences.

Seen through the framework of trees along the sidewalk, withdrawn and demure behind their neat front gardens, these houses give scale to the grandeur of Lord Street, offset the ostentation with their homeliness and humility yet add to the architectural dignity and elegance.

There are just thirteen private houses left on Lord Street, all on the inland side. Eight of them are at the west end of the street, all together

*Wellington Parade, 6 to 20 Lord Street, an attractive Regency terrace, built in 1817-1818.*
*[photo, Cedric Greenwood]*

in a pleasing Regency terrace, nos. 6 to 20 Lord Street, variously known in the past as Wellington Buildings, Wellington Parade and Wellington Terrace.

Built in 1817-18, these are the oldest buildings on Lord Street, Wellington Parade has the air of the Regency terraces of London, Brighton and Cheltenham, although we cannot pretend it is as magnificent or beautiful. The houses have round-headed doorways with fanlights, canted bay windows and a delicate Graeco-Italian flavour with their refined proportions and stucco facades.

No. 16 is the only one that still has its original ground floor bay windows with their tall, slender frames and Tudor arches. No. 12 has graceful semi-elliptical alcoves in the lounge and No. 10 has been completely remodelled inside with semicircular alcoves flanking a beautiful Louis XIV moulded fireplace, Adam mouldings on the ceiling and pelmets and wrought iron balustrading on the stairway.

The cottage-like fronts belie suprisingly roomy houses inside. The stout old purlins along the roof of the terrace are reputed to be from an old shipwreck on the Southport shore.

In 1820 the terrace was mentioned in a description of Southport in Longman's 'Guide to all the Watering and Sea-Bathing Places'. It read: 'Southport . . . dates its origin within the last 40 years; at present it forms a considerable village, comprising numerous neat cottages, most of them of recent erection; those elevated on an embankment called Wellington Terrace are very handsome.'

And John Gregson, of Manchester, gives us an idea of the kind of people who lived in this terrace in his sketch of Southport life composed in verse and published in the *Liverpool Kaleidoscope* in 1824:

> 'The castellated towers of Belmont frown
> On what, or whom? The thrifty sons of trade
> Who hold abode in Wellington Parade.'

The remaining five houses on Lord Street are at the east end,

***Above:*** *Best preserved of the Regency houses at the east end of Lord Street is No. 156, built in about 1827, with Tudor arch windows that were characteristic of Southport Regency. It is probably the only building on Lord Street to have been converted back from an office to a house.*
*[photo,* Southport Visiter.*]*

***Left:*** *Trinity Cottage, near Holy Trinity Church, No. 19 Manchester Road, one of several Regency houses in this vicinity.*
*[photo, Cedric Greenwood]*

*Semi-detached Regency Gothick: Mount Cambria, 23 and 25 Manchester Road. [photo, Cedric Greenwood]*

*This detail of Mount Cambria shows the late-Gothic or Tudor arch porch with its battlements and pinnacles and the Tudor arch fanlight divided by tracery into two smaller Tudor arches. In the foreground is a sundial. [photo,* Southport Visiter.*]*

interspersed between others that have been converted into offices, on the block between Hill Street and Union Street, built about 1827.

Most of them have been altered beyond recognition and the best preserved is no. 156 Lord Street, which retains its original narrow Tudor arch windows and is now fitted with shutters. It was originally Spring Lodge.

The Bold Hotel, built about 1830 on the corner of Lord Street and Seabank Road, is a more classic, if undistinguished, piece of Regency. Its wooden portico with coupled Doric pillars underlines the Greek lineage of Regency architecture. The hotel also has plain Regency flush windows, canted bay windows and a parapet. The name is characteristically moulded in a relief panel on the Seabank Road side: THE BOLD FAMILY HOTEL. — note the full stop.

The remaining extant Regency houses of early Southport stand around the corner from the east end of Lord Street, along the downtown end of Manchester Road.

When the moon rides high and peers through the tall treees rustling in the wind and the huge shadow of the magnificent Gothic tower of Holy Trinity Church falls across their Gothic features, the houses from 19 to 29 Manchester Road, with their narrow Tudor arch windows and their wooden porches with battlements and pinnacles, look just the setting for a ghost story. By day their Regency delicacy is delightful and, withdrawn behind their bosky front gardens and sub-tropical foliage, they take on an enchanting, dreamy atmosphere as if they exist in an oasis of time past. They were built in the period from 1842 to 1852 in the eastward extension of the town over the Starr Hills—the sandhills of marram grass.

Trinity Cottage (no. 19), a double-fronted detached house, was built in 1842, followed by Mount Cambria (nos. 23 and 25), a semi-detached pair of double-fronted houses, and Heaton Mount (nos. 27 and 29), a

*Horsfield Cottage, 4 Lord Street West, was built in 1835, a pleasing single-storey villa in the Regency Gothick idiom with a low-pitched roof and a parapet. In the early 1970s Southport Town Council agreed to its demolition for a block of flats. Then the Government listed it; now it is a rest home.*
*[photo,* Southport Visiter.*]*

*A classic Regency house, No. 9 Manchester Road, with its weeping elm on an oval lawn.*
*[photo,* Southport Visiter.*]*

*Titus Cottage and Roach Villas, 43-47 Aughton Road, Birkdale, were built in about 1858; the matching single-storey extension on the right was added in 1956.*
*[photo, Cedric Greenwood]*

*3 Westcliffe Road, Birkdale. [photo, Cedric Greenwood]*

*The Bowling Pavilion in the Botanic Gardens, Churchtown. [photo, Cedric Greenwood]*

straight semi.

All are faced in stucco and the late-Gothic or Tudor details are expressed in characteristic Regency simplicity and charm. In addition to the Tudor windows there are rectangular, stepped Tudor hood mouldings over the flush windows and Tudor arch fanlights instead of the normal Regency semi-circular fanlights.

At Trinity Cottage, as becomes its name, the fanlight comprises three arch windows side by side. At Mount Cambria and Heaton Mount the main arch of the fanlight is divided by tracery into two smaller arches.

Only Mount Cambria features the embattled and pinnacled porches and only no. 27 retains the beautiful semi-elliptical archway linking the front and back rooms. The arch is decorated with floral mouldings and supported by two ornate moulded imposts.

Nos. 31 and 33 Manchester Road also have Tudor arch windows on the first floor and small classical pediments.

Down the road, no. 7, built in 1837, is a double-fronted detached house very like Trinity Cottage with Tudor windows and hood mouldings but its stucco facing has been replaced with roughcast.

It has a Venetian doorway, Tudor arch panels in the door and the fanlight tracery is an artistic design of interlaced Tudor arches. Inside, the house has recently been tastefully refitted with moulded friezes and Adam style fireplaces.

Next door, no. 9 Manchester Road is a classic Regency house, foursquare with a parapet half hiding a low-pitched roof, faced in white stucco with no mouldings—just pure, clean, classical simplicity and elegant design.

It was built in 1835 and is fronted by a weeping elm on an oval lawn. The delicate lace-like white iron railings that ran atop the low front wall were unfortunately removed for World War Two. The old coach house and stables still stand at the end of the back garden, fronting on to Walton Street.

In Birkdale there are five Regency Gothick style houses, at 3 Westcliffe Road, 6 Lulworth Road and 43-47 Aughton Road, but they are of the Victorian period, not of the Regency period, being built in the 1850s. The group of three in Aughton Road comprises Titus Cottage (no. 43) and Roach Villas (nos. 45 and 47), built about 1858. Although built some 30 years out of their time, they faithfully reproduce the characteristics of the period with Tudor arches, broad mullions and stepped hood mouldings. No. 47 has a matching extension built in 1956. This charming group is quite different from anything else in the street.

Finally, let us look at the handsome classical bowling pavilion in Botanic Gardens. It was built by Southport Corporation in 1938 but the design is attributed to the late Peter Fleetwood Hesketh, who emulated the late-Regency architect Decimus Burton. A deep colonnade with white Doric columns under a pitched and hipped roof frames a building with a semi-elliptical central doorway and Tudor arched windows sub-divided into pointed Gothic tracery of mullions and glazing bars. This fenestration extends to the lavatory windows at the back.

——— o OOO o ———

Chapter Four

# *Railway Stations*

THE trains don't exactly go through the middle of the house, as in the words of the song, but it feels like it. They pass 4 feet 6 inches from the front door at 57A Portland Street. This narrow, two-up, two-down house hard by the tracks at Portland Street crossing was Southport's first railway terminus, from 1848 to 1850. Although it is not an architectural piece, it is historically interesting and was spot-listed in 1988 as a building of significance in the development of Southport. It is also interesting in that the design and style of this cottage was standard for all station houses along the Liverpool, Crosby and Southport railway when it opened in 1848.

The original southern terminus was Waterloo and the railway company ran horse buses between Waterloo and Liverpool until the line was extended to Liverpool Tithebarn Street terminus in 1850 (later called Liverpool Exchange).

James Whitehead wrote in the *Southport Guardian* in 1894, in his series 'Recollections of Southport 50 years ago', about a ride in a third-class open truck with no seats from Portland Street to Waterloo in 1848 and, according to him, there was also a station at Duke Street.

Presumably, the ex-railway house that still stands at 49A Duke Street was the station house because it stands in the same position relative to the railway and road as Portland Street house and is the same design, with the stone tablet over the door for the inscription of the station name, although it stands further back from the track.

It is purely conjecture but Duke Street may even have antedated Portland Street as the Southport terminus temporarily to open the line earlier, before extension to Portland Street, because Duke Street was the first road the railway crossed that led into town in 1848. At Portland Street and Duke Street, Southport has the only two surviving original houses of the Liverpool, Crosby and Southport Railway.

The old Birkdale Station was sited about 300 yards down the line from Hillside Station, between Sheringham Road and Dunkirk Road, which was the nearest point on the railway to old Birkdale village around the corner of Liverpool Road and Sandon Road.

This station served Birkdale for just three years, until 1851 when it was succeeded by the present Birkdale Station at the end of Weld Road

*Southport's first railway terminus: Portland Street, 1848. [photo,* Southport Visiter.*]*

to serve the growing new residential area of Birkdale Park, which was begun in 1850. Hillside station was not opened till 1926; it was named after Hillside Farm at that point on the edge of the sandhills.

The tablet provided for the station name at Portland Street was never inscribed. The station was open only two years before the line was extended to a new terminus at Eastbank Street in 1850 but the house at Portland Street crossing remained the stationmaster's residence. The final extension to Chapel Street terminus followed in 1851. The tablet on Duke Street station house was not inscribed either, but the tablet on the old Birkdale station house, inscribed 'Birkdale Station', remained as a memorial tablet to the station until the house was demolished in 1968—117 years after the station closed.

Whitehead says that the old Southport terminus at Portland Street used to stand on a cinder cart track surrounded by meadows on the outskirts of the town. The station house stood at one end of a long, narrow, wooden platform, just 1 foot 6 inches above the trackbed, with no shelter for passengers. The small brick annexe abutting on to the street used to be the booking office.

Some effort was made by the Liverpool, Crosby and Southport Railway Company to make the plain, functional station house a little architectural, with a Perpendicular Gothic arch over the doorway and rounded-off brickwork around the door and windows.

The double-fronted house is only one room deep—one up, one down, each side of the front door with a reverse staircase leading up from the back corner of the left-hand room. It contains a stone 200-gallon water tank that collected water off the roof.

The house is now home to Southport Model Railway Society so trains now run through the middle of the house too. The society rents the house from British Railways and was responsible for its spot-listing in 1988. The buffs hope to open it to the public as a permanent model railway exhibition with a museum of railway relics in the old booking office.

In front of the house is the eighteenth milepost from Liverpool with cast-iron figures on a wood board. It stands on the edge of what looks like a low platform built of sleepers. If this was the original platform, it was only 2 feet 7 inches wide in front of the house.

Duke Street station house, although basically the same design, has an Early English Gothic arch over the door and normal squared-off brickwork around the apertures. The entrance had double doors, like a station booking hall, until the house was sold and modernised. Both houses were tenanted by successive generations of railwaymen until recently.

Southport has had twenty-two railway stations in its history. Five company lines converged on the town between 1848 and 1887 and in the second half of the nineteenth century Southport grew to be the third largest seaside resort in Britain, after Brighton and Great Yarmouth, it was larger even than Blackpool.

Between 1887 and 1901, lines radiated from four terminals in the town centre: Chapel Street for Liverpool Exchange, London Street for Wigan and Manchester Victoria, Central (in Derby Road) for Preston and Downholland, and Lord Street for Liverpool Central, Warrington, Manchester Central and Stockport.

Between 1926 and 1938, Southport had sixteen stations open simultaneously: Chapel Street, Birkdale, Hillside, Ainsdale; St. Luke's, Blowick; Hesketh Park, Churchtown, Crossens; Lord Street, Birkdale Palace, Ainsdale Beach, Woodvale; Meols Cop, Butts Lane, Kew Gardens.

Today the five lines that converged on Southport have been reduced to two, from Liverpool Central (low level) and Manchester Victoria, and the sixteen stations have been whittled down to five: Southport (formerly Chapel Street), Birkdale, Hillside, Ainsdale and Meols Cop.

The most complete of these is Birkdale Station. The gabled glazed canopies, which once ran almost the full length of the platforms, have been shortened to six bays on the down platform and four bays on the up side, giving it the character of a small country town station rather than a suburban one.

The centrally placed cast-iron columns along the middle of the platforms, the frilly wooden valances, the redbrick buildings with stone architraves, the glazed wooden coamings over the steps to the pedestrian subway and the long, weatherboarded, cantilevered signal

*This was Lord Street railway terminus from 1884 until 1952 and Southport bus and coach station from 1954 to 1987. [photo. Cyril Loker]*

cabin complete a pleasant Victorian period railway station set.

The only extant original Southport terminus is Lord Street station. This steepled and symmetrical Victorian building once sported a glazed canopy over the forecourt, but latter-day trappings marred the ground-floor elevation. The great cast iron and glass train shed of 1883 was pulled down in 1989 for a new shopping centre. The buildings were stripped and gutted for restoration, which was to include a new canopy. Then work stopped and, at the time of writing, the future is uncertain.

Lord Street Station, opened in 1884, was the grandiose terminus and headquarters of the Southport and Cheshire Lines Extension Railway, which ran fourteen and a half miles to Aintree Central, where it joined the Cheshire Lines system, giving through workings.

The SCLER was promoted by a group of local worthies who owned land they wished to develop in Birkdale and Ainsdale. The line from Aintree headed across open fens via nowhere and approached Southport through the coastal dunes at Ainsdale and Birkdale, where the company hoped to develop seaside resorts.

Between Lord Street Station goods yard and Birkdale Palace Station they laid out a seafront for Birkdale: Rotten Row, Birkdale Recreation Ground (now Victoria Park) and the Esplanade. Ainsdale-on-Sea Station, later called Ainsdale Beach, gave rise to a hotel with a boating lake next to the station and a Promenade of gaunt boarding houses with the Lido and gardens on the seaward side.

The line was owned by the SCLER but operated by the Cheshire Lines Committee, a joint committee of the Great Northern, Midland and Great Central Railways, with trains of CLC brown coaches hauled by Great Central green engines and sometimes by Midland red engines.

It was thirty one and a half miles from Southport to Liverpool and forty nine and a half miles from Southport to Manchester by the Cheshire Lines route, compared with eighteen and a half miles to Liverpool and thirty-five and a half miles to Manchester by the Lancashire and Yorkshire Railway. However, trains from Lord Street gave direct connections at Manchester and Stockport with trains to all parts of the Great Central, Midland and Great Northern systems and in the summer there were through coaches from Lord Street to Sheffield, Lincoln, London, Bournemouth, Norwich and Lowestoft over the ramifications of those systems.

Lord Street station goods yard was right next to Victoria Park and handy for the Great Flower Show when it began in 1924. At flower show time the yard was busy with special trains of exhibitors and equestrians with vans of plants and rocks and horseboxes.

By 1950 traffic had declined to five departures and six arrivals at Lord Street on weekdays, to and from Liverpool and Manchester, and no trains on Sundays. The railway closed in 1952 but the station reopened in 1954 as the Ribble bus and coach station.

North Western, which took over Ribble buses in south-west Lancashire in 1986, closed the bus station in 1987 and it was bought by Sibec Developments for part of a ten acre, £80 million shopping centre to be called the Winter Gardens (The former Winter Gardens adjoined the east side of the station and stretched to Coronation Walk. The complex comprised a conservatory, opera house, theatre, circus, aquarium and gardens.)

The developers have demolished the train shed to build a larger one in cast iron and glass 500 feet long, 100 feet wide and 80 feet high to cover the new shopping mall. The new cast iron and glass structure is intended to echo both the old station and the Winter Gardens conservatory and the elevational drawings show banded brick walls with piers and recessed arches that should look more like a railway station on the Duke Street and Kingsway sides than the old station did.

The contractors, who also had a stake in the redevelopment, pulled out in 1990, leaving the building a derelict ruin and Sibec to look for another partner and contractor in less prosperous times than those when the scheme was begun. If the shopping scheme is abandoned, the building would make a fine suite of municipal buildings to replace the rabbit warren of council offices in Eastbank Street and Coronation Walk and the space behind it would make a fine bus and coach station and multi-storey car park, both of which the town sorely needs more than shops.

______ o OOO o ______

Chapter Five

# *Portland Hall*

THE Georgian-style house at 41 Portland Street is unique in Southport. Its placid, classical façade veils the most chequered and interesting history of any building in the town. The house and the adjoining hall behind it were originally Southport's first museum and subsequently a concert hall, a theatre, a skating rink, a newspaper office and works, a drill hall and a furniture store. The Rt. Hon. William Gladstone, four times Prime Minister of Great Britain, used the concert hall at 41 Portland Street as his platform for a great political speech the year before he first became Prime Minister.

Although built in 1863, more than thirty years after the period of architecture to which it belongs, the house is a classic piece of Georgian architecture with its low-pitched triangular gable end, or pediment, over the front, its moulded window cases, its rusticated quoins and its trussed pediment over the Venetian doorway, which has an attractive architrave of delicate Adam style mouldings of recent origin in place of the former fanlight.

It is not only its architectural style that makes this house unique. It is really little more than a façade—38 feet wide but only 22 feet deep—to the hall behind. It was formerly the foyer and offices. The hall in which all the history took place is only 84 feet long and 36 feet wide.

It was opened in 1863 as the Royal Museum of natural history. The front of the house carried the royal coat of arms and the gate piers were surmounted by bronze elephants. The hall of the museum was filled with glass cases of stuffed animals and birds, fossils and shells. The walls and ceiling were hung with African, Indian and Oriental weapons. At the far end of the hall were an aviary and an aquarium.

A special attraction at the opening of the museum was a live nshigo, a species of mammal between a chimpanzee and a gorilla. It was the first nshigo to be seen in England and it was reported to show a startling likeness to human beings with its smooth face, its black hair, whiskers and beard, its upright and gentle deportment and its relatively high degree of intelligence.

The Royal Museum was not a financial success and was converted in 1867 to the Royal Music Hall. It was on December 19th of that year

*No. 41 Portland Street. Behind the Georgian façade, a chequered history. [photo, Cedric Greenwood]*

that Gladstone, who was M.P. for South Lancashire, addressed a packed meeting in the hall on the issues of the time; the Abyssinian war, electoral reform, education and the Irish troubles. He received a great ovation and was cheered on every point he made throughout his speech.

The music hall was not, as is commonly understood by the term, a comedy theatre but a concert hall for serious musical performances. In 1871, under new ownership, it was renamed the Concert and Assembly Rooms. Concerts gradually gave way to opera and the English Lyric Opera and Burlesque Company gave a series of 'refined and classic entertainments'.

In turn, opera gave way to drama. The Amphitheatre Star Company presented plays there in 1871—a year before the hall was given its theatre licence.

In 1874 the place was renamed the Vaudeville Theatre. The *Southport Visiter* of June 27th 1874, described it as an 'elegant drawing room theatre . . . visited by the elite of Southport'. Tragedy, burlesque and farce walked its boards.

In 1877 the Winter Gardens band pavilion was granted a theatre licence and this much more commodious and attractive theatre meant the end of the Vaudeville and the end of the more colourful era of the history of 41 Portland Street.

In the late 1870s it became one of Southport's several successive roller skating halls. In the early 1880s it was the office and works of the *Southport Daily News*. In the late '80s it was the headquarters and drill hall of the Royal Naval Artillery Volunteers. In 1890 it became a furniture warehouse.

It was at this stage—27 years after it was built—that the Georgian 'façade' first became a residence. Ben Purser, owner of the furniture store, lived there. He was a cabinet maker, venetian blind manufacturer and furniture remover with a shop on Lord Street.

The Depository, as the premises were called, was not a very becoming address for a private residence and a gracious Georgian house, and in 1905 he renamed the place Portland Hall. This impressive name was really a revival of its colloquial term of reference when it was an assembly hall, a skating hall and a drill hall.

Down through two take-overs in the furniture removal business, no. 41 Portland Street remained a furniture warehouse until 1988, when it was sold to Anthony and Glenys Sheldon, who will make it their private residence with an indoor swimming pool, as yet another use of the historic hall.

Chapter Six

# *Victorian Villas*

AS a town that is largely the creation of the Victorian age and the home or place of retirement of many of Liverpool's and Manchester's wealthiest kings of commerce and industry and merchant princes, Southport has many stately Victorian villas hidden behind the tree-lined highways and bosky front gardens of Scarisbrick New Road, Hesketh Park and Birkdale Park.

Birkdale Park was the name given by Thomas Weld Blundell when he decided, in 1847, to develop Aindow's Hills, the sandhills seaward of the railway at Birkdale, as a high-class residential estate of 'marine residences'. Up to that time Southport, which grew up around the mouth of the Nile and Nile Square (now Lord Street West), ended abruptly at the town boundary at the west end of Lord Street West, the manor of Birkdale being a separate domain until it merged with Southport in 1912.

Mr. Weld Blundell was a member of the Weld family of Lulworth, in Dorset, who were distantly related to the Blundells of Ince Blundell, near Crosby, and inherited the Blundell estates, including the manors of Birkdale and Ainsdale, when the male line of the Blundells, which had lasted for 658 years, ended in 1837. Thomas Weld also inherited the additional surname Blundell according to the terms of the will of Charles Robert Blundell. From this piece of history we have acquired the names Weld Road, Lulworth Road, Blundell Avenue and Blundell Drive in Birkdale.

Mr. Weld Blundell secured powers for the development of Birkdale Park by Act of Parliament in 1848. On October 13th that year the *Liverpool Mercury* reported: 'The township will be laid out under the superintendence of eminent surveyors and landscape gardeners so that the plan will meet the views as well of those who would wish to possess marine residence of considerable extent as of those who would desire to erect single houses or shops. We do not despair of shortly seeing the healthy locality covered with beautiful residences suitable for the habitation of the most respectable parties.'

John Aughton, a builder who had come from Preston to Southport, started developing Birkdale Park in 1850. He worked at it until 1854, when he left to take up a big railway contract in Canada. Aughton

*Birkdale Lodge, 1 Lulworth Road, an Italianate villa built in 1850.*
*[photo,* Southport Visiter.*]*

Road is named after him.

Fashion in architecture had shifted from Regency to Italianate by the 1850s. This is strongly in evidence in the first houses John Aughton built in Birkdale Park, with low-pitched roofs, prominent gables and eaves and Roman-arch windows.

By 1866, Mannex's Directory of Southport said of Birkdale: 'The buildings are generally on a scale of grandeur and magnificence superior to those of Southport and many of them are occupied by opulent merchants and manufacturers from Liverpool and Manchester as well as by other wealthy and highly respectable persons. The streets are asphalted and laid out with much taste and elegance.'

Through the reverse curves of Lord Street West we enter Birkdale Park at the expansive fork junction of Lulworth Road and Westcliffe Road, flanked by three fine stuccoed Italianate villas built in 1850 – John Aughton's noble beginning of his estate. On the left is Birkdale Lodge, 1 Lulworth Road, on the right 6 Westcliffe Road and Sunnymede School up a drive behind it.

Birkdale Lodge, at first sight over the hedge, looks like a Victorian Gothic villa but this is only because of the steep pitch of the spire on

*The stairway in the panelled hall at Birkdale Lodge. [photo,* Southport Visiter.*]*

the tower. The hood mouldings, smartly picked out in black against the white walls, also smack of Gothic. But if the pitch of that spire was as low as the pitch of the roof, Birkdale Lodge would be a classic Italianate villa, with its prominent overhanging eaves forming pediments, its Roman arches and its shallow, arched recess in the west wall.

Not unnaturally, most of the houses John Aughton built in Birkdale Park are in the same style, although they are all quite different in design and use segmental as well as Roman arches. It seems that he—or his architect if he had one—unwittingly set a vernacular style of domestic architecture, for a great many of the houses built in Southport and Birkdale in the latter half of the nineteenth century have the same low roof, pediments, prominent eaves, Roman and segmental arches, arched recesses and arched window tracery that we see in Birkdale Park. Because of this strong Italian influence, Gothic never got a real hold on domestic architecture in Southport.

To return to Birkdale Lodge, there is a surprise in store for anyone entering it for the first time. Right in the centre of the house is a great oak hall, like the hall of a Tudor manor house, rising the full height of the house. It is panelled and half-timbered with a magnificent carved

No 6 Westcliffe Road, Birkdale.
[photo, Cedric Greenwood]

oak fireplace, stained glass windows on the stairway and a galleried landing. It's like the set for a period play: because of its central position in the house the doors of all the rooms open on to the hall. One door, in the corner of the hall, leads into a pleasant cast-iron and glass conservatory. There is also a coach house, now a garage.

Birkdale Lodge was a 'gentlemen's academy', a day and boarding school, for some years during the second half of the nineteenth century.

Across the way, no. 6 Westcliffe Road has similar canted bay windows on the ground floor but is otherwise strongly classical in its treatment, with pilasters, pediments, rusticated quoins and trussed eaves. This villa, named Westcliffe, was the first house to be built in Westcliffe Road, to which it gave its name. We shall return to this house later to have a close look at its ornate cast iron portico.

Sunnymede School, tucked out of sight behind no. 6, is not a feature of the street scene but its stuccoed, rusticated Italianate tower is a prominent feature of the skyline as viewed from the beach. It matches the tower of the Royal Clifton Hotel nearby to give the town an Italianate flavour on its seaward aspect. This villa was named Wyborne Gate and doubled as a private house and a 'ladies' boarding school' in Victorian times.

St. Wyburn, a massive Victorian villa in ponderous Italianate at 26 Westcliffe Road, Birkdale.
[photo, Cedric Greenwood]

Two more of John Aughton's stuccoed Italianate villas are nos. 2 and 4 Gloucester Road, built in 1851. Although detached, they were built as a pair, one being a mirror image of the other. The Romanesque porticos are on facing sides of the projecting central bay on each of these otherwise symmetrical houses.

Gloucester Road contains several other early houses of Birkdale Park with Roman arch windows and glazing bars characteristic of John Aughton.

*The porch at Hollinwood.*
*[photo,* Southport Visiter.*]*

*These beautiful stained glass windows flood the stairway with coloured light.*
*[photo,* Southport Visiter.*]*

Westcliffe Road contains the largest and most imposing Victorian villas. Many of them have been private schools and some still are. St. Wyburn at no. 26 is an immense house, very Italianate with its low-pitched roof, prominent eaves and Romanesque windows. It is built in red brick with a heavy stone portico on Tuscan columns, stone bow windows on the ground floor, stone architraves and quoins. The panelled wooden cornice is a feature.

St. Wyburn was built in 1866 as Helenshome, the home of a stockbroker. It was renamed St. Wyburn in 1903 and remained in use as a private house until 1938, when it became a school.

Of the relatively few Victorian Gothic villas built in Southport there are a number along Cambridge Road and a notable group on a short section of Scarisbrick New Road north of Ash Street. They are huge, dark and forbidding, with Early English pointed arches and baroque ornamentation. Some have square central towers. They belong to a fantasy world of follies, sham ruins and haunted houses.

Opposite those on Scarisbrick New Road stands one of the most handsome examples of Victorian domestic architecture in Southport, quite different in style from its Gothic contemporaries and different again from Birkdale Lodge, built thirty years earlier. This is Hollinwood, No. 35 Scarisbrick New Road, built about 1880 as Dudley House, the residence of Mr Samuel Campbell Hulton Sadler, Deputy Clerk of the Peace for Lancashire at that time.

It is built, like all the best houses in Southport, in glazed red Accrington brick and hard yellow sandstone from the Pennines. Its beautiful features are the stone bow windows, the arcaded balustrading over the square bay windows, the curved gables and, not least, the porch.

*Hollinwood, 35 Scarisbrick New Road, built in about 1880. [photo,* Southport Visiter.*]*

The porch has a double Roman arch: an outer arch in sandstone and an inner arch in polished black marble. It is flanked by two polished marble columns with Renaissance Ionic capitals. Under the apex of the arch is a carving of two herons and a dog in flowing lines.

A touch of Scottish baronial and fairy-tale castle architecture was lavished on Southport by the Romantic school of Victorian architects in the last thirty-five years of the nineteenth century with the building of large, noble hotels and villas sporting semi-circular towers and turrets with conical spires.

The first of these towers appeared in the 1865 extension of the Royal Hotel on the Promenade. The architecture of the extension west of the portico—the graceful, flowing lines of the Roman arch windows and curved glass—is notably different from the plainer architecture of the original part of the hotel built only twelve years earlier on the corner of Coronation Walk.

The Prince of Wales Hotel, built in 1877, has two circular towers on its Portland Street side. One is a four-storey tower with a cute little dormer window in the spire. The other is a first and second floor turret on the corner of King Street.

Three tower houses were built on Park Crescent in the 1870s and

*The graceful, flowing lines of the semi-circular towers, Roman-arch windows and curved glazing in the 1865 extension of the Royal Hotel (now the Royal Clifton Hotel) on the Promenade. [photo,* Southport Visiter.*]*

they are all identical: Studley Court on the corner of Argyle Road, Salfordian old people's home on the corner of Brocklebank Road and Hatherlow House, another old people's home on the corner of Park Avenue.

The most noble of the semi-circular towers take us back to Birkdale Park. Kingswood, 13 Westcliffe Road, built about 1872, is now an independent school for boys. In addition to its tower it has a handsome classical portico of yellow sandstone and magnificent oak panelling and carvings throughout the interior.

The tower sections of these palatial piles built in the 1860s and '70s are really semicircular bay window projections on the front elevations and in every case the architecture of the windows on each floor is different.

Window surrounds are in stucco, red brick, yellow sandstone and

*Note the difference in the architecture of the windows on each floor of the semi-circular tower at Kingswood, 13 Westcliffe Road, Birkdale. [photo,* Southport Visiter.*]*

wood. Many of the windows are divided by stone pillars with ornate capitals.

Not only is the window architecture different on each floor but in many cases the relieving arches and hood mouldings over them are variations on the actual shapes of the windows. There are segmental, semi-circular and trefoil arch windows with pointed arches over the top. There are square-headed windows with segmental, pointed and trefoil arches.

The work of the Victorian architect was surely a labour of love.

There appears to have been a lapse in building semi-circular towers from the late 1870s through to the late 1890s, when they reappeared as threequarter projections or bastions on the corners of buildings and this time they were not window projections but more for effect; they were nearly all brickwork with few, narrow windows, which seemed to

***Above:*** *One of a pair of early John Aughton houses in Birkdale Park: Woodlands, 4 Gloucester Road, built in 1851.*
*[photo, Cedric Greenwood]*
***Above, right:*** *John Aughton-style Roman-arched glazing bars at 22 Gloucester Road, Birkdale.*
*[photo, Cedric Greenwood]*

***Right:*** *Normanhurst, 15 Lord Street West, has a façade which is quite unique in Southport, in an indefinable, free style of architecture. It is a symmetrical composition of semi-circular arches, balustrading, corbels and terra-cotta decoration with stepped gables capped by semi-circular pediments. Formerly a private residence, it was a hotel from 1925 until 1960 and is now divided into apartments. Date unknown, but probably around 1889.*
*[photo, Cedric Greenwood]*

be merely there to provide the minimum light inside the towers.

There is a particularly fortress-like one on the villa at no. 3 Grosvenor Road, Birkdale. It is almost devoid of windows—just a vertical line of narrow, almost arrow-slit, apertures, the rest of the tower face being broken up with ribbing and corbelling. This tower houses a cosy little ante-room on each floor.

*No. 3 Grosvenor Road, Birkdale. [photo, Cedric Greenwood]*

*No. 5 Grosvenor Road was saved from demolition. [photo, Cedric Greenwood]*

The house also has a square, spired turret, some half-timbering, ornate mouldings on the coving under the square spire and on the frieze over the front door and carved trefoil arches in the yellow sandstone frieze. This large house, built in 1897, was modestly named

Hame (northern dialectial for 'home').

The house next door, 5 Grosvenor Road, has no circular tower but appears to have been built by the same architect as no. 3 to judge from its deep moulded cornice. It also features stained glass windows over the main portal with a moulding of the Liver bird in the tympanum of the pediment above and pyramid roofs over the squared bays.

The demolition men had already occupied this house when it was saved by an emergency conservation order for this western corner of Birkdale Park in 1988.

Our tour of selected Victorian villas ends in the eastern corner of Birkdale Park to look at two villas of more imaginative and original design.

The house at 23 Gloucester Road, built in 1892, is quite different from any other in Southport with its three-gabled upper storey cantilevered forward of the ground floor the full width of the house. The projection is carried by the wide window bays, rounded-off at the corners.

Each floor has a strong cornice line, as have the three gables. The gables are hung with semicircular tiles and the projecting upper storey has three modest ranges of windows—one under each gable—divided by glazing bars into small panes, like the equally neat window bays below.

In the otherwise symmetrical facade, the steps lead up from the right to a front door offset to the left under a semi-elliptical carved stone arch. Inside, carved wooden Tudor arches lead from the hall into the lounge, a large, sumptuous room with a deep frieze of foliage mouldings and wooden English Ionic columns framing a cosy inglenook.

*The unique and highly distinctive 23 Gloucester Road. [photo, Cedric Greenwood]*

*12 and 14 York Road. [photo, Cedric Greenwood]*

While all the Victorian villas we have looked at were designed in the grand manner of the period, we come, finally, to one of the minority that were modestly designed in a quaint, picturesque style and this is my favourite house in Southport: 12 and 14 York Road.

Although now two houses, it was originally one and has to be looked at as one composition—a lively, varied, non-symmetrical composition of oriel windows, decorative woodwork and reverse curves. Observe also the matching reverse curves of the porch arch and the trusses under the oriel windows. The tall finials in wood and cast iron give a flourishing finish.

The original house of 1857 extended from the hexagonal tower at the right hand corner to the first oriel window. The left hand end of the house—left of the brick pier—with the corner oriel window forming an Emetty circular turret and the cute little oriel bow window on the ground floor, was an extension of 1916, enhancing the overall composition in the spirit of the original.

From 1896 to 1938 this house was the Owen College of Physical Education for women PE teachers, taught by a German system with music. The foundations of the gymnasium are under the back garden; beyond that were tennis courts. Although a Victorian villa and a college, the original part of the building, now no. 12, makes a delightfully cosy home because of its small scale, the irregular layout of corridors and rooms, graceful semi-elliptical arches throughout the house, solid woodwork and some arched windows with a myriad small panes divided by thick glazing bars.

Chapter Seven

# *Promenade Hospital*

AS you look at Southport from the sea—or from the pier—the most prominent and distinguished building in Southport's façade is a flamboyant assemblage of masonry, gables and spires like a French chateau. It is the Promenade Hospital.

A free mixture of French Gothic, Flemish and Elizabethan styles, it pierces the skyline with its octagonal steeples, its embattled, stepped gables and its groups of tall, hexagonal chimneys.

In close-up it takes on the guise of an Oxford college with its ornate fretwork of yellow stone, which breaks up the mass of glazed red Accrington brick.

The main feature of this ornamentation is the corbel table of long, vertical, stone fins, with segmental arches under the eaves, like machicolations under a castle parapet, which hood pairs of windows at regular intervals. The vertical lines of these corbel fins are continued in the ornate stone framework over the dormer gables.

Most of the windows on the three floors below the eaves have segmental arches too but those in the dormer windows on the front and in the stepped gable ends have trefoil arches.

Even the hopper heads on the downspouts—which all bear the date 1882—are decorated with tiny battlements. The architects were Paull and Bonella.

Paradoxically, this ornate building is the newer part of the hospital, while the plain, two-storey building on the Seabank Road side is the older part. The 'new wing', as this major part of the hospital was modestly called at the time, was built from 1880 to 1883 at a cost of £30,000—part of the surplus of the Lancashire Cotton Famine Relief Fund. This fund was for the relief of distress in the mill towns during the paralysis in the cotton industry caused by the American Civil War and the stoppage of cotton supplies. The hospital was a convalescent home exclusively for people from the mill towns.

Although the older part of the hospital bears the date 1806, it was not in fact built until 1853. The year 1806 was the date of the foundation of the Strangers Charity, which built it.

Subscribers to the Strangers' Charity could nominate each year one

***Above:** The Promenade Hospital, seen from the west. [photo, Cedric Greenwood]*

***Left:** This detail of the Promenade Hospital shows the corbel table of long stone fins under the eaves, the ornate stone framework over a dormer gable, trefoil arches over the former windows, a group of four hexagonal chimneys and an embattled hopper head on a downspout with the date 1882. [photo,* Southport Visiter.*]*

'sick, poor stranger' to spend three weeks at Southport. As the Charity had no hospital or home of its own for many years it merely paid the 'strangers' limited expenses for board and lodging in the town.

The Charity built a 'dispensary' on Lord Street, near Coronation Walk, in 1823. It housed the office, the subscribers' meeting room, a surgery and hot and cold sea-water baths.

In 1853 the charity built more commodious premises where Seabank Road ran down to the shore. It was called the North Meols Local Dispensary. This was the foundation of the Promenade Hospital.

The first accommodation for the charity's patients was provided in the extensions of 1862, when the place was renamed the Southport Convalescent Hospital and Sea Bathing Infirmary.

As the name of the charity indicated, this hospital was for 'strangers' from other parts of the country, not for Southport people, and the major extension in the 1880s was for people from the cotton mill towns. It remained so—with the exception of the two world war periods, when it was commandeered as a military hospital—right up to 1948 when, under the National Health Act, it became part of the local hospital service and was renamed the Promenade Hospital.

The older part of the hospital housed the spinal injuries unit, the X-ray department, a geriatric ward, the gymnasium and doctors' quarters. The 'new wing' was the main part of the hospital, housing geriatric and orthopaedic and spinal patients, an operating theatre, an out-patients' department and a pharmacy.

At one time, the hospital had more than 200 beds. It closed in April 1990 in the reorganisation of Southport hospitals with the development of the new District General Hospital on Blowick Moss.

It will be interesting to see what, if any, new use can be found for this listed building because it is so vast. It is the kind of building that on Blackpool sea front would be a conference hotel or a convalescent home. Nothing of the architectural inspiration for the exterior is reflected in the typically institutional Victorian interior, which will be no loss and can only be improved by conversion but externally this spendid architectural pile would be a great loss if it disappeared from Southport sea front.

——— o OOO o ———

Chapter Eight

# *Lord Street Medley*

IF Lord Street were all Tudor and Elizabethan half-timbered buildings like Eastgate Street, Chester, or all classical stonework like Grey Street, Newcastle-on-Tyne, wouldn't it be fine? Yes, but wouldn't the overall effect be too heavy and rather incongruous for a seaside resort?

It is the variety of architecture—the unplanned medley of shapes, sizes and styles—that spices the Lord Street scene. As a Victorian town this is inevitable.

Victorian architects were repelled by the ugliness and squalor of the Industrial Revolution. They turned their back on this new world and its new materials, they turned the clock back to earlier, nobler ages—ages when things were made by artist-craftsmen and not by machines.

With the vigour and enthusiasm that were endemic in the Victorian age, the architects evoked all the past styles, Gothic, Tudor, Elizabethan, Jacobean and classical, together with assorted styles from overseas like Flemish, Greek, Italian and Muslim.

Generally speaking, they used romantic architecure (the Gothic, Tudor, Elizabethan and Jacobean) for ecclesiastical and scholastic buildings and classical architecture (the neo-Greek, neo-Roman, Palladian, Queen Anne and Georgian) for commercial and public buildings like banks and town halls.

The Victorians built many fine examples of the styles they revived and the nineteenth century saw the erection of more of the world's finest buildings than any century had ever seen or is ever likely to see.

Unfortunately, owing to the popularity of the romantic movement for its escapism from current social evils, architecture fell into less academic and less aesthetic hands than those of the very able architects who masterminded the revivals. Ornamentation, instead of being a means to an end, became an end in itself and it is a pity that a number of poor imitation, hybrid, fantasy styles gave Victorian architecture a bad name.

Southport has a mixture of good, bad and indifferent Victorian architecture in every past and foreign style listed above. We shall look at the romantic buildings in this chapter and the classical in the next.

In a short stroll through central Lord Street we find amazing variety, probably not found in so short a compass anywhere else. At the risk of steering a collision course through the throng on the sidewalk, it is a rewarding and uplifting experience to raise your sights above your fellow pedestrians, the passing traffic and the shop fronts and take an objective look at the architecture around you.

Every time you pass along a street you notice more details, you become more aware of your environment and your footslogging peregrinations around town become more interesting and pleasurable.

Along our shopping blocks the ground storeys now present faceless sheets of glass—as much display space as possible—but above the colonnades and the canopies the old façades remain for the most part unchanged, with all their nineteenth-century pillars, arches, mouldings, cornices, pediments and finials.

We have a Muslim building at 319-25 Lord Street, next door to the Midland Bank, although I doubt if many people have noticed it. It almost baffles description in English architectural terms, for Muslim

*Ornate gables, mouldings, stone bands and oriel windows above 247-9 Lord Street.*
*[photo,* Southport Visiter.*]*

*Muslim architecture, 319-325 Lord Street. [photo, Cedric Greenwood]*

architecture—alias Arabian, Islamic, Mohammedan and Saracenic—is indigenous to Spain, North Africa, Turkey, Persia and India. Its characteristic round and pointed horseshoe arch windows and complex patterns in moulded brick are to be seen in this building, which also used to sport a pointed horseshoe cupola, but this disappeared about 1911.

On the other side of the Midland Bank, Dunn's building has some ornate mouldings over the first floor oriel window and in the gable, which incorporates two panels of moulded encaustic tiles and is flanked by a balustraded parapet with vase-topped piers like the adjoining bank.

Next, the tall four-gabled Albany Buildings, built in 1884, are the most outstanding example in Southport of Victorian romantic ornamental architecture, incorporating Early English Gothic stone windows and Tudor-Elizabethan half-timbered gables.

However distasteful these fancy, romantic revival styles may be to

*Late-Victorian ornamentation reaches its height in this range of buildings from 335 to 355 Lord Street. G. A. Dunn & Company (left), the Albany Buildings (centre) and the Lakeland Sheepskin Centre (right). Note the austerity where oriel windows have been replaced with flush windows. [photo, Cedric Greenwood]*

the purists and classicists, when you observe the austere surrounds of the flush windows which later generations have substituted for the old oriel windows on some of the first floor façades of both the Albany Buildings and the Muslim Building, then you begin to appreciate the efforts of Victorian architects in decorating buildings.

Look at the moulded yellow, encaustic tiled pillars flanking the windows under the Elizabethan gables of the Albany Buildings and the carved woodwork of that Elizabethan balcony high above the street. (The other half-timbered gable was similar originally but has been cut back to form an open balcony.)

Out of the melting pot of borrowed styles an original Victorian style evolved in the last twenty years of the Victorian period. It has been called, for want of a better name, Commercial Classic, but it is not to be confused with classical commercial architecture. It was generally applied to commercial buildings but it was not the classical architecture of the Greek and Roman orders.

This was, indeed, a happy marriage of the two distinct schools of architecture of the period, an artistic blend of the classical and the romantic. It might almost be called the Norman Shaw style because that eminent London architect was the author of the movement in the early 1880s with such buildings as his New Scotland Yard.

In sum, Commercial Classic was a free-style combination of Jacobean and Wren, a composition of Jacobean roofs, chimneys, gables, oriel windows and turrets carried on broad semi-circular Romanesque arches with Wren cupolas, niches and small circular windows. It spawned the Art Nouveau movement in domestic architecture that followed in the Edwardian period.

There is a little Commercial Classic gem next door to the Albany Buildings: the façade above the Lakeland Sheepskin Centre at 355-57 Lord Street, built in 1900-1. Contrast its smooth lines and graceful

***Above:*** *The noble National Westminster Bank (late Westminster Bank) on London Square is characteristic Victorian Commercial Classic. This photograph was taken before the ground floor windows were modernised. [photo,* Southport Visiter.*]*

***Left:*** *The red sandstone edifice of the former Manchester & County Bank above the shop canopies in Lord Street. [photo, Cedric Greenwood]*

beauty with the severity of the romantic Albany Buildings.

The finest and most characteristic example of Commercial Classic in Southport is the National Westminster Bank (late Westminster Bank) on the corner of St. George's Place and London Street, that noble pile of yellow sandstone that forms a fitting backdrop to monumental London Square. It was built in 1892 by Parr's Banking Company, of Warrington. In 1918 it became the London County, Westminster and Parr's Bank, in 1923 the Westminster Bank and in 1970 the National Westminster Bank.

Note the carved stonework of the window mullions and transoms, the niche that breaks up a blank space in the London Street frontage, the carved stone foliage around the circular windows in the gables and note the gable finials: pillared niches surmounted by sitting lions.

The architect, William Owen, of Warrington, was renowned for his woodwork and the banking hall featured very fine mahogany panelling and a carved mahogany fireplace under a beautiful ceiling of massive, ornate, moulded plaster beam casings supported by fluted square pillars. All this has disappeared in successive modernisations in the 1960s, '70s and '80s. I wonder if the old panelling and ceiling are still there to be discovered and restored one day when man grows tired of his clinical surroundings.

The new false ceiling at the level of the window transoms has led to the removal of the unusual carved stone mullions and transoms in the 1973 modernisation and their replacement with full-width glazing and stainless steel panels that fill in the Roman arches above transom level. I have illustrated the bank as it was before the external modernisation, for comparison.

*Victorian fantasy in terra cotta and encaustic tiles above Hammick's bookshop. [photo, Cedric Greenwood]*

Proceeding east along Lord Street we come to the only two Southport buildings in local red sandstone. One is Bridgford's estate agency (late Ball & Percival), 132 Lord Street, built at the same time as the Lakeland Sheepskin edifice, 1901, again in Commercial Classic, with beautiful semi-elliptical and semi-circular arched windows on the ground floor and carved stonework similar to both the Lakeland Sheepskin Centre and the National Westminster Bank.

The other red sandstone building, almost opposite, at 423 Lord Street, is the former Manchester and County Bank, a lively Commercial Classic composition of steep-pitched roofs, dormer gables and oriel windows of the first and second storeys above the shop canopies, its banking hall and entrance modestly tucked away up a side alley. The bank was built in 1892 and closed by amalgamation in 1952. The ornate banking hall remained in a time warp behind the shops in use as a corn and seed merchants' office and store till 1981 then in disuse till 1985, when it was discovered and converted to Lombard's licensed restaurant.

The banking hall has been restored and adapted in an imaginative three-level design, tastefully executed, complete with the bank coat of arms in a mosaic floor, the clock above the fireplace, panelled walls, moulded frieze and ceiling and a beautiful ochre tinted pattern of autumn foliage in the stained glass skylight.

_______ o OOO o _______

Chapter Nine

# *Classical—The Halls of the Gods*

THE most beautiful architecture ever evolved was that of the classical era, approximately 1620 to 1830, the golden age of British architecture, although we have to thank the ancient Greeks and Romans for its origins and the early-fifteenth-century Italians for its renaissance.

Commercial and public buildings continued to be built in classical Palladian, Baroque and Greek styles through the romantic, Gothic nineteenth century to the mid-1920s and it was in buildings of this kind that Southport architecture reached its zenith.

Classical architecture was both solid and elegant, with an air of security and serenity. An impressive building was the status symbol of a company in the nineteenth century and early-twentieth century and banking companies invoked the Classical Renaissance to symbolise security. They spared nothing in lavishing the finest materials and craftsmanship on their buildings to show the capital on which their businesses were founded and to attract the best customers. The banks are the most distinguished class of buildings in Southport and its suburbs. Generally speaking they are more architectural, both outside and in, than the churches.

Walk around the banks of Southport and your footsteps echo through the noble halls of all the ancient Greek and Roman orders of architecture: Doric, Ionic, Corinthian and Tuscan—each a system of rules governing the proportions and styles of columns, bases, capitals and entablatures.

To my mind the most magnificent building in Southport is the Midland Bank on Lord Street. Designed by Southport architect, Ernest W. Johnson, who had his

*Roman Corinthian magnificence. The Midland Bank, Lord Street, built 1888-89. It is even more magnificent inside. [photo, Cedric Greenwood]*

office in the neighbouring Albany Buildings, and built in 1888-9, this bank is acknowledged as one of the finest Roman Corinthian buildings in northern England.

The windowless façade is a beautifully balanced composition of polished pink granite columns and pilasters and yellow sandstone pediments and carvings with a balustraded parapet. It is a façade full of three-dimensional interest, well regulated in proportion to the size of the building.

Coupled columns support the main triangular pediment framing the portal—a Roman arch surmounted by a smaller triangular pediment. The rest of the façade is covered in beautifully carved spandrels, trusses, cornices, tympanums and decorative panels and neatly edged and squared off with pilasters up the corners. The Midland Bank sign

*The red marble Roman Corinthian columns, the baroque cornice and the ornate moulded modillions in the great hall of the Midland Bank. [photo, Cyril Loker]*

covers the carved frieze of the main pediment.

The building is even more magnificent inside. The great banking hall is awesome in its gargantuan proportions and its beauty and richness of ornamentation and colour with its massive, soaring, deep-red marble Roman Corinthian columns, their gilded acanthus leaf capitals, the baroque cornice and ornate moulded modillions to the skylight cornice, the beige wall panels and the mahogany counters. A giant vaulted skylight fills the great hall with natural light. Above all, it is an enriching and ennobling experience. It is a pity that security has necessitated the recent addition of the tall, reinforced glass screen along the counter, which splits the banking hall in half and detracts from the former open aspect and spaciousness of the hall.

In passing between the façade and the banking hall don't miss the vestibule with its Roman arches, one on top of the other, sheathed in green and purple moulded encaustic tiles, and its barrel vaulted ceiling with ochre and white mouldings.

The North Meols Savings Bank opened at Churchtown in 1837 but the Midland has the oldest genealogy of Southport banks. It goes back to the Preston Banking Company, which opened a branch here in September, 1857. It was this company that built the magnificent Corinthian edifice on Lord Street in 1888-89—the name Preston Bank is still inscribed in the frieze over the portal—and in 1894 it was incorporated into the London City and Midland Bank, now the Midland Bank.

*Like a Grecian temple, the Ionic portal of the National Westminster Bank (late District Bank) at 253 Lord Street, built 1920-24.*
*[photo, Cedric Greenwood]*

The oldest customers at the bank were J. Connard and Son Ltd., the Lord Street jewellers, whose account dates back to 1884—Preston Company days—and it was they who supplied the carved wooden clock on the east wall of the banking hall when the company opened its new building five years later.

It is interesting to note that the other principal classical banks in Southport were built in the 1920s. After the romanticism that was predominant in the Victorian era there was a resurgence of classical building and the renaissance finished with a flourish in the first thirty years of this century.

The National Westminster Bank (late District Bank) at 253 Lord Street is like a Grecian temple in white Portland stone. The façade is one vast Greek Ionic portal with a massive bronze door in a beautifully carved stone architrave. It was built from 1920 to 1924 and the honours for this building go to Francis Jones of Manchester.

Evidently modern generations of bankers do not set the same store by classical architecture as a symbol of security or to impress customers as did the founders of the banking companies. In 1972 there was a plan to replace the Portland stone curtain wall of this portico and the bronze door with a glass wall and a glass door in a stainless steel doorcase.

Opposition saved the portico but the rest of the modernisation scheme swept away the classical banking hall or, rather, covered it up as in the other National Westminster Bank we saw in the last chapter. A false ceiling hides the coffered ceiling and glass dome skylight while the Renaissance Ionic pilasters and Roman arches have been boarded up in modern cladding and the marble floor has been carpeted.

The District Bank was formerly the Manchester and Liverpool District Bank. This company first established a branch in Southport in 1884, taking over the premises of the defunct Southport and West Lancashire Bank (built 1879) on the corner of Lord Street and Eastbank Street.

The old banking hall is now part of the Atkinson Central Library but few of the hundreds of people who sit in there daily ever notice the beautifully coffered ceiling with massive, ornate beam casings and the pattern of panel mouldings all in white, against the wedgwood blue panels. The old bank fireplace is still there too.

To return to the 1920s, Barclays Bank (late Martin's Bank) at 14 Eastbank Street, in polished red granite Roman Ionic, was built in 1925. Polished red granite and Roman Ionic are beautiful to see anywhere but one cannot help feeling that the choice of stone and architecture here are a bit heavy for such a small building.

*A ceiling many of us sit under but few of us notice—in the reading room of the Atkinson Library. This room was formerly the banking hall of the Southport and West Lancashire Bank (1879) and its successor, the Manchester and Liverpool District Bank. [photo,* Southport Visiter.*]*

Barclays Bank (late Martin's Bank) at 365 Lord Street is also red granite. It was built in 1905 as the Bank of Liverpool and is one of the rare applications of the Tuscan order in Southport. Tuscan is of Roman origin, being added by Vitruvius about 30 B.C. to the adopted Greek orders. Alas, here again, the classical grandeur and grace is lost on such a small building but, as if in an attempt to counter this, the polish on the granite on both Martin's Banks brings out the architecture beautifully.

Both these small red-granite banks have closed as a result of the take-over by Barclay's. The Lord Street branch closed in 1978 but remained in use by the banking company for storage until 1981. Then it became The Old Bank restaurant and now it is a women's dress shop called Happit. The Eastbank Street branch closed in October, 1988, and has been disused. At the time of going to press there were plans to demolish the building for shops.

Generally speaking, in the economic conditions after World War

*Mighty Palladian in Portland stone—the former National Westminster Bank (late National Provincial Bank) is the key building in the town centre, dominating London Square at the corner of Lord Street and Nevill Street. It is pictured here when it was still a bank. It is now a bookshop, with carefully enlarged windows on the ground-floor elevation. [photo, Cedric Greenwood]*

One, classical architecture was not as rich and ornate as it was before the war. It was plain and simplified. The former National Provincial Bank next door to Martin's Bank, at 367 Lord Street, was an exception. Built from 1925 to 1927, this mighty Palladian edifice of rusticated stonework and engaged Renaissance Doric columns with a Baroque cartouche over the main door, all in white Portland stone, is a superlative cornerstone to the finest block of buildings in Southport and the key building in the town centre.

In 1970 the National Provincial Bank was amalgamated with the Westminster Bank and the District Bank to form the National Westminster Bank. The new company then had three banks on Lord Street and the former National Provincial was the casualty. It closed in 1972 and the ground floor bank was then used as a wine bar.

The bar and the commercial offices above were closed in 1988 and have been converted to a two-storey bookshop, Sherratt and Hughes. To alter a classical bank to a shop without spoiling its architectural character is not an easy exercise. The modest, rusticated ground floor windows have been widened and deepened on the Lord Street front and deepened on the Nevill Street side.

The more characteristic plainness of the 1920s is shown in Lloyd's Bank opposite. This was the last of the great classical banks built in Southport, from 1927 to 1928. Its plain first, second and third floor façade is offset by rustication up the corner section, trim fluted Greek Ionic pilasters dividing the windows of the banking hall and a heavy cornice with carved modillions. The mansard roof with dormer windows, which is an authentic feature of domestic classical architecture, is also characteristic of classical commercial buildings of the 1920s.

The banking hall has an ornate coffered ceiling with fluting along the sides of the beam casings and moulded modillions and panel mouldings. The beams are supported by Composite capitals on plain, square pillars and pilasters.

The Composite order is a combination of the Renaissance Ionic and Corinthian orders, added by the Italian Renaissance architect Andrea Palladio (1518-80) when he published his works on the correct rules of classical proportions. Inigo Jones, who was appointed chief architect to the English Crown in 1615, had studied Palladio's works in Italy and through him Palladian architecture became the basis of the Italian Renaissance in England.

We do not have any strict Palladian buildings in Southport but we do have one or two of Palladian influence and character. The National Provincial Bank is one. The Town Hall is another. It is Southport's 'White House', seat of local government, attractively finished in white stucco, as was much of Southport at the time it was built, in 1852-4. It is a modest size Town Hall for a town like Southport—the municipal offices are scattered all over the central area—but it was big enough for Southport in its time.

Against a rusticated, pilastered façade, terraced steps, lit by globular lamps, lead up to the portal of Greek Doric columns flanked by coupled square pillars supporting an entablature and a balcony. From the balcony, engaged Roman Ionic columns and coupled pilasters lead the eye up to the pediment with a tympanum which is, as it should be, the crowning glory of the edifice: a beautiful carving in bold relief of the figures of Justice, Mercy and Truth, picked out in white against a Wedgwood blue ground and gilded. The façade is finished off with an arcaded parapet.

The Town Hall is less pleasing inside. Although classical in design and detail, it is bereft of classical grandeur or grace; Victorian austerity belies its date and the new decor does not pick out the potential of the classical features and mouldings.

The Council Chamber is a gem: a charming little Regency style House of Commons with well-marked grain in the wood pews and dado panelling, pastel-green walls and vaulted ceiling, white moulded trusses, cornices and beam cases. I like the two stout green columns, fluted only halfway up, with gilt-edged white Composite capitals supporting a beautiful semi-elliptical arch, outlined in white, framing the public gallery. There is a matching arch over a recess in the wall where the Mayor and council officers sit.

The original borough coat of arms, with an open lifeboat manned by four oarsmen and a coxswain in souwesters, can be seen in the stained glass window in the vestibule of the chamber and carved in the head of the Mayor's high seat and the pew ends in the chamber. This coat of arms lasted from the borough's incorporation in 1867 until 1923, when the College of Heralds substituted a heraldic thirteenth-century armed merchant ship of the Cinque Ports for the lifeboat.

*Southport Town Hall (1852-54) in all its chaste classical beauty. [photo, Cedric Greenwood]*

Thomas Withnell was the architect to the Town Hall. He also built the town's first Market Hall on London Street (1848 to 1857), the North Meols Local Dispensary (1853, now the oldest part of the Promenade Hospital) and the Royal Hotel (1853-54).

The ballroom of the Royal Hotel, now the Royal Clifton Hotel, was a rich and regal piece of classicism with the panelled walls broken at regular intervals by Roman arch doorways and windows and Renaissance Ionic pilasters, a cornice decorated with dentils and the vaulted ceiling, but, like the Town Hall, the richness and regal character has been lost in the new decor.

In one corner of the ballroom is an enclave with a stage for the dance band. It is a small threequarter rotunda with a low domed ceiling and horizontally oval windows. The wall and ceiling are panelled with mouldings.

The twilight of the architecture of the gods came with the dark portents of and prologue to World War Two and Southport's final monument to the classical age was the Law Courts building, incorporating the Police and Fire Stations, built on the corner of

Albert Road and Manchester Road from 1938 to 1940.

The building is the 1930s' translation of the spirit of the classical age. It is built to classical proportions in red brick and white Portland stone. The horizontal lines of rustication in the stone ground floor storey of the Law Courts—the projecting central section of the building—is continued as stone ribbing around the red-brick Police and Fire Stations at each end, which have stone plinths and portals. Roman columns with Tuscan bases and simplified Corinthian capitals stand sentinel at the tall portal of the Law Courts.

The great marble hall is the feature of this building. It is imposing without being ostentatious. The walls and floor are of white marble tinted yellow ochre and brown. Octagonal pillars clad in dark green marble with fascinating markings and modified Corinthian capitals with gilded acanthus leaves stand at the four corners of the hall and others support two bridges linking rooms on the upper floor. Light oak panelled doors lead to the many rooms of the hall and globular lamps hang down from the ceiling.

It is one of those halls in which every footfall, cough and vocal sound is echoed, people talk in hushed tones and the raised voices of lawyers in the courtroom off the hall are the only voices that are really heard.

Around the walls of the hall are gilded circular plaques with bas relief profiles of great lawyers of history from the 13th century until three years before the Law Courts were opened. The last of them, Sir Frederick Pollock, had a great lifespan, from 1845 to 1937, in which he must have witnessed the greatest changes in the history of the world.

To me the most interesting part of the hall is the floor. You can stoop and see masses of fossils of shellfish and other marine creatures entombed in the marble. Geology is a side interest of architecture.

The Law Courts were built only fifty years ago at a cost of £116,000, but since then rising costs of labour and materials have put an end to building in the grand manner and beautiful Olympian edifices like this, the Midland Bank, the District Bank and the National Provinicial Bank will never rise again.

Chapter Ten

# *Cast iron*

ALTHOUGH Victorian architects spent much of their time reviving Gothic, Greek and other old styles, there was one great architectural phenomenon that was all their own and belonged to no other age, before or since. It is something for which Southport is well known. This was the revolutionary phenomenon of building in cast iron and glass, one of the more aesthetic products of the Industrial Revolution with its delicate, lace-like construction, which manifested itself in structures like Crystal Palace and the great arch roof of St. Pancras Station.

Southport and Lord Street are famous, if nothing else, for the cast iron and glass colonnades along the shop fronts on the seaward side of the street. They run in an almost continuous chain for three quarters of a mile from one end of the street to the other, broken only in a few places by side streets, banks, the Bold Hotel and buildings of the 1930s and '60s with cantilevered canopies. They provide an umbrella for shoppers in the rain in much the same way as the rows of Chester.

Lord Street's iron colonnades were erected between 1860 and 1900 and most of them were made in Glasgow iron foundries. They all bear the name of one of the following eight ironfounders embossed in the ironwork at the bases of the columns: James Allan Snr. & Son, Glasgow; Falkirk Iron Co., Falkirk; David King & Sons, Glasgow; J. & A. Law, Glasgow; McDowall, Steven & Co., Glasgow; W. Macfarlane & Co., Glasgow; J. Monk, Preston; George Smith & Co., Glasgow.

The columns, besides holding the canopies up, also carry the rainwater down from the guttering atop the canopy fascias.

Some of the canopies on the central and eastern sections of Lord Street have curved glazing bars, giving a graceful arched effect, and some have been replaced by the more conventional straight glazing with a more severe appearance.

By about 1980 many of the colonnades were showing signs of age and neglect and some of them, far from providing an umbrella for shoppers, were leaking rainwater in cascades. Skylights darkened under moss and guano and panes of glass were replaced by sheet metal. The rain leaked through because the drain systems were blocked. The hanging baskets of flowers on summer days were augmented all the year round with tussocks of grass and weeds sprouting from the gutterings filled with moss and guano.

Cascades of rainwater streaked the ornate ironwork with rust and corroded the steel lintels and glazing bars. Successive coats of paint no longer covered up the rust and the cracks. The corner columns, which doubled as downspouts, filled up with water because of blocked outlets and cracked in the frost. The blockages were caused by the highway department raising the level of the footpath over the years.

Restoration began in 1979 with the colonnade on Tower Buildings at the corner of Leicester Street thanks to a conservation-minded landlord. Since 1980, grants under the Town Scheme from the borough council, the former county council and the Department of the

*Cast-iron colonnade at T. R. Highton's furniture shop, 129-131 Lord Street. [photo, Cedric Greenwood]*

*Cast-iron colonnade at G. A. Dunn's, the men's hatters and outfitters, 333 Lord Street. [photo, Cedric Greenwood]*

Environment, administered locally by the Town Hall, have seen the progressive restoration of most of Lord Street's iron colonnades.

Restoration involves new steel lintels and glazing bars, re-casting damaged iron spandrels, frills and pediments in moulds taken from corresponding original parts and stripping the rest of the ironwork by hand-scraping, caustic bathing or grit blasting to reveal the decorative mouldings hidden under umpteen coats of paint. Holes are filled with resin and the bare iron is treated with various long-term protections against rust. Unless restoration is done properly and unless the landlords or their tenants maintain the drainage systems, then the trouble will recur.

Russell & Bromley's colonnade at the corner of Nevill Street was new in 1973, when the shoe shop took over from Alexander's fashion shop. The new owners converted a plain cantilevered canopy into an iron colonnade using spiral iron columns characteristic of the South Eastern & Chatham Railway from Frant station in Kent and adding wrought-iron foliated spandrels.

The architectural highlight of the Lord Street shop colonnades is the barrel-vaulted portico of Wayfarers Arcade, built in 1898. The tenants of the arcade clubbed together to make this portico the second restoration job, in 1980, and the whole arcade is gradually being restored in phases.

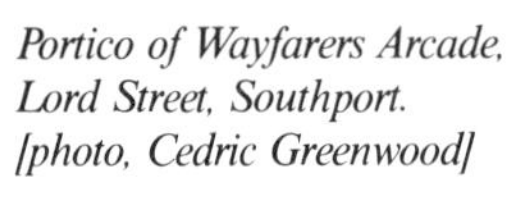

*Portico of Wayfarers Arcade, Lord Street, Southport. [photo, Cedric Greenwood]*

This arcade is also the highlight of the Lord Street shopping experience—a unique Victorian shopping precinct. The modest entrance tunnel leads to a surprise inner sanctum, a cast-iron and glass cathedral or conservatory of Victoriana that is a haven from the wind, rain and motor traffic.

It is an enclave of beautiful things: merchandise of top-quality designs and workmanship in elegant shop windows of turned mahogany in a setting of potted palms and ferns, a running waterfall into a goldfish pond with giant lilies and soft orchestral music overhead. There is also a gallery of shops upstairs with stained-glass arched transom windows. When I last visited, there were sprays of flowers tied with ribbons around the balustrade along the balcony. Observe also the moudled frieze under the glass dome. The beautiful portico and splendid dome and skylight of this arcade are the work of Walter Macfarlane of the Saracen Foundry, Possilpark, Glasgow, one of the largest firms in the cast iron industry, which exported prefabricated buildings, verandahs, balconies, gates, railings, bandstands and fountains all over the world and made its mark on the British Empire.

The arcade was opened in 1898 as Leyland Arcade, named after the

*Inner sanctum of the Wayfarers Arcade, built in 1898. [photo, Cyril Loker.]*

Liberal MP of the time. The name is still seen in the floor at the entrance. Originally there was a bandstand and an aquarium. It became Burton Arcade in 1950 and Wayfarers' Arcade in 1976, named after successive leaseholders.

The late Arthur Jacobson, pop recording star of 1928-33, dancing violinist and conductor of palm court orchestras, had the municipal dance orchestra at the Floral Hall and Lord Street bandstand in 1935-41 and 1948-49 and finished up as leader of a three-piece orchestra in the arcade from 1950 to 1959.

The Lord Street bandstand, in which he played, was a classical

*Lord Street's new bandstand, built in 1985 in Victorian style between Market Street and Eastbank Street. [photo, Cyril Loker.]*

dome on columns surrounded by continental-style cafe tables under colourful sunshades in a stone-balustraded arena in front of the municipal buildings. That was demolished in 1969 to be replaced by a cubist concrete 'cascade' in some rather trivial formal gardens with concrete becks.

The classical bandstand had beautiful proportions and replaced a rather mean-looking Victorian iron bandstand. In 1985, in a revival of interest in brass bands, Victoriana and the restoration of the iron colonnades along the shop fronts, a handsome new Victorian-style cast-iron and steel bandstand was built in Lord Street between Eastbank Street and Market Street.

It was designed for the borough council by Southport restoration and landscape architect Martin Perry, octagonal in plan with prominent eaves. The lacy spandrels, the capitals and bases of the steel columns and the balustrading were cast from patterns taken from the extant bandstands in Victoria Park, Southport, and Derby Park, Bootle. It stands on an octagonal, panelled plinth of reconstituted stone resembling Portland stone.

The new bandstand is a remarkable reflowering of Victorian cast ironwork. It was initiated as a local monument to Marks & Spencers' centenary in 1984 and intended to be part of a remodelled piazza or gardens in front of the civic buildings, to stand between the Arts Centre and the Atkinson Library. The bandstand can be dismantled

*Top:* *A magnificent ornate white iron portico with a carriage gable at 6 Westcliffe Road, Birkdale.*
*[photo, Cedric Greenwood]*
*And below is the cast-iron verandah on Drayton House, 2 Lulworth Road, Birkdale.*
*[photo, Cedric Greenwood]*

and re-erected and Marks & Spencer, the Civic Society, the bands and public opinion favour resiting it there when municipal funds run to remodelling the gardens between Market Street and Christ Church.

It was in porticos that iron and glass architecture in Southport reached its height. They recall the gracious leisurely days of horsedrawn carriages, top hats and crinolines, for as 'porte-cocheres' they were the coach entrances of our larger Victorian hotels and villas, being built out to the carriageway to protect the passengers from the rain.

There are two fine examples of domestic coach porticos opposite each other on the fork junction of Lulworth Road and Westcliffe Road in Birkdale. No. 6 Westcliffe Road, built in 1850, has a magnificently ornate white iron portico with a hipped roof and a carriage gable supported by eight slender spiral columns. This portico is unusual in being fitted with rolling wood shutters designed to be pulled down in grooves between the columns to keep the wind out if required.

Drayton House, at 2 Lulworth Road, also built in 1850, has a barrel-vaulted portico, guarded by hexagonal lanterns, at the head of a circular driveway within the apex of the fork road junction. This house has two main entrances, the iron portico being the one for carriage passengers and the classical brick and stone porch on the Lulworth Road front being for pedestrians. The two entrances are linked by a cast-iron verandah around the corner of the house. The ironwork probably post-dated these houses by about thirty years.

_______ o OOO o _______

Chapter Eleven

# *Art Nouveau*

THE twentieth century began with a new architecture, the Art Nouveau, or new art. It was part of a wider movement covering the whole field of arts, not just the three-dimensional, and it attracted architects who reacted against the structural revolution of steel-framed buildings and reinforced concrete, harked back to traditional styles, materials and methods of construction and held that architecture was an art not a science.

Art Nouveau architecture was formative in the late 1890s. It seemed to take its inspiration from Shaw's Commercial Classic but was almost entirely domestic and an artistic free style based on Tudor and Elizabethan cottages, applied to large houses.

Its leaders were C. F. A. Voysey (1857 to 1941), Charles Mackintosh (1869 to 1928) and Sir Edward Lutyens (1869 to 1944), who together built a stylish bridge between Victorianism and twentieth-century-modern. Art Nouveau flourished in the period 1900 to 1910 and had faded out in this country by 1914, although it continued to find favour on the continent for many years.

As an art form, colour and texture were more important than ornament. Materials were red-brick, half-timbering and roughcast. Each house was individually designed an artistic non-symmetrical composition of steep-pitched roofs, often flared to prominent, overhanging eaves, tall chinmeys, sometimes in clusters, large expanses of plain walls punctured by modest mullioned windows. Rooflines and gables were often carried down to the ground floor to give a large house more of a cottage appearance, and the walls of the more extravagant designs sported flared butresses just for style.

Additional features of Art Nouveau houses in Southport are stone mullioned windows in groups of three, angular bays, oriel windows with no projecting masonry below the sills, small circular windows like portholes, decorative mouldings in the gable elevations, segmental bow windows on the ground floor – sometimes forming three-quarter circular bastions on corners, wide semi-circular arched porches, often with short convex pillars, and Tudor arches inside.

The plain walls are broken up by strong horizontal lines of string courses incorporating hood mouldings over the windows and the windows themselves, although tall and narrow, ranged in horizontal lines.

The designs strike a fine balance between the vertical and horizontal

*Abbeyfield, 74 Scarisbrick New Road, a nursing home since 1972.*
*[photo, Cedric Greenwood]*

*No. 15 Rutland Road.*
*[photo, Cedric Greenwood]*

*Dunblane, 50 Cambridge Road, built in 1899.*
*[photo,* Southport Visiter.*]*

elements and in the proportions of wall space and windows. This was the art of the Art Nouveau architect.

Art Nouveau houses are to be found in only two habitats in Southport: Cambridge Road/Hesketh Road and Scarisbrick New Road/Rutland Road, where the middle and upper classes could still afford architects to design their houses.

They were built along the south side of Cambridge Road and the west side of Scarisbrick New Road only, the houses opposite being Victorian. These roads must have been an odd sight at the end of the nineteenth century with the Victorian houses on one side and open fields on the other, although there were some thatched cottages in Cambridge Road.

Specifically, Art Nouveau houses were built along the even numbered side of Cambridge Road in odd groups, with infilling, between 1899 and 1910. Today, mean postwar pink-brick houses break up the continuous line of Art Nouveau, which are to be found at 2-50, 66-68, 78-90, 94-108 and 114-132.

They were built along the even-numbered side of Scarisbrick New Road from 64 to 90 progressively from 1905 to 1910, along both sides of Rutland Road from 1 to 15 in 1905-9 and along the even numbered side of Hesketh Road from 2 to 42 in 1907-8. There is also some Art Nouveau influence in Coudray Road, Rawlinson Road and Brocklebank Road but no real examples of the style.

The best examples of the new art in architecture are to be seen at 28 and 50 Cambridge Road, 10 Hesketh Road, 74 and 90 Scarisbrick New Road and 15 Rutland Road.

*28 Cambridge Road.*
*[photo, Cedric Greenwood]*

Note the large stained glass windows above the front doors at 2 and 4 Cambridge Road. These two and no. 50 were among the first Art Nouveau houses to be built in Southport, in 1889 to 1901, and illustrate the transition from Victorian to the new Edwardian style. No. 50 has a matching extension at the side added in the 1930s. The entrance hall leads to a central staircase under an arch on convex pillars.

Nos. 8 and 10 Hesketh Road, evidently by the same architect, are offset at an angle to the road half facing each other in a shallow V-formation and feature red sandstone architraves and fin-like mullions. No. 8 has a low portico on massive red standstone blocks, a wood-panelled hall and Art Nouveau stained-glass windows.

The finest example of Art Nouveau in its final flourish is no. 28 Cambridge Rd, built in 1909-10 in the style of C. F. A. Voysey. If it was not designed by the great man himself—and he did not list it among his works—it is a remarkably good copy. Other architects and builders copied his designs and this house is characteristic with its flared roof and buttresses, prominent eaves, horizontal lines and modest windows. The front of the house is a fine and pleasing composition.

*The K Shoe Shop in Chapel Street is one of the most handsome buildings in the town centre.*
*[photo, Cedric Greenwood]*

There is one commercial building in Southport in this style and a very fine example too: the elevation above the K Shoe Shop (formerly Macfisheries) in Chapel Street. To my mind this is one of the most handsome buildings in the town centre with its restrained bowed and mullioned windows, the little Saxon window at the top and its gracefully-curved Dutch gable. It was built at the beginning of the period, 1899-1900.

Chapter Twelve

# *Neo-Tudor half-timbering*

GLIMPSED between the trees, it looks like one of Nelson's 'wooden walls of England', come to berth alongside Lord Street with its towering stern overhanging the sidewalk. Behind the veil of foliage stands a bit of old Chester. It is the only completely half-timbered building in Southport—as outstanding an example of Elizabethan half-timbering to be found anywhere as it is singular in the otherwise brick and stone façade of Lord Street.

The four-storey building at 215-17 Lord Street used to house a high-class fashion store (originally Lomas's, later Cannell's). It was empty for several years during the 1960s and since 1970 it has had a succession of owners, mostly discount stores, interspersed with periods of emptiness.

Ornate half-timbered panelling below the windows on the first and second floors was boarded over with advertising fascias, a van knocked off the Waverley Street end of the colonnade and neglect of routine building maintenance led to decay of the fabric. In 1979 the colonnade was restored and the building repainted but the neglect went on.

Today the building is resplendently restored. That achievement is a monument to the energetic and irrepressible former borough conservation officer (1975-87), Mr Michael King, who persevered in persuading the tenants on a repair lease to part with some cash and take a fifty per cent Town Scheme grant to give our wooden ship a thorough refit to architects' specifications, which saw the restoration of the ornate panelling on the front.

It is the mass of timberwork and leaded glass and, in particular, the bulky oriel windows on the second floor that give the building its eighteenth century nautical flavour. Underneath, on the first floor, is a range of oriel windows with ogee (reverse curve) arches, trefoil arches and ornate carved spandrels.

Above, on the third floor, are twin gables, one incorporating a covered balcony, the other with an open balcony around it. The tall spike finials on the gables give a stylish finish to the building. The whole place is strongly reminiscent of the college barges on the Isis at

Looking like one of Nelton's 'wooden walls of England', 215-17 Lord Street has been splendidly restored.
*[photo, Cedric Greenwood]*

Oxford.

It is the work of a Southport architect, James E. Sanders, and was built in 1903 in the Tudor Revival, which began in the 1880s and lasted into the 1930s.

The difference between original Tudor and neo-Tudor, apart from the age, is that while the timberwork is the framework of genuine Tudor buildings (1485 to 1603) it is only a decorative facing on the latter-day Tudor style buildings. Improved forms of construction have evolved since Tudor times.

It would be wrong to give the impression that all Tudor buildings were of half-timber construction. In fact, most of them were built of red brick or stone but in the well-wooded lowlands of west and south Lancashire, the West Midlands and the south-eastern counties oak-framed buildings were the rule.

Along the coastal lowlands of Cheshire and Lancashire from the Wirral to the Fylde is a unique belt of Tudor-Elizabethan revival architecture with warm-red glazed Accrington brick ground floor walls and black-and-white half-timbered upper works.

Apart from the lone Elizabethan building on Lord Street and, of course, the countless striped gables in the houses of the 1920s the Tudor revival in Southport manifested itself in large residences in the Hesketh Park district and Birkdale. I have picked two houses, one in

*Neglect and decay of the neo-Elizabethan half-timbered building on Lord Street, photographed about 1985. Vegetation blocks the guttering of the colonnade.*
*[photo,* Southport Visiter.*]*

*The oak hall of Rosefield Hall is lined with 216 oak panels, each of which has a different design in carved tracery. [photo, Cyril Loker.]*

each district, as examples.

One is No. 40 Hesketh Road, which was built about 1908 as Hermon's Hill, the home of Baron de Forest. It is now Rosefield Hall and was given this name by Mr George Rose who went to live there in 1929 and founded the Garrick Theatre on Lord Street in 1932 (now the Top Rank bingo hall).

It is believed that Mr Rose added the beautiful carved oak tracery to the panelling in the main hall, which is the feature of the house. There are 216 panels in the hall and the tracery on every one is different!

George Rose also added the rose mouldings around the bargeboards of the porch. The house is rich in ornate mouldings inside. As you enter the porch you are faced with a niche with a shell arch and Ionic pilasters. This is a prelude to the beauties to come: the carved oak-panelled hall, the magnificent walnut-panelled dining room with fluted Ionic pilasters, a bedroom with delicate Adam-style mouldings and another bedroom that is a fantasy of heavy 'icing sugar' mouldings on the walls, ceiling and the seventeenth-century-style ceiling-high fireplace.

The other example of Tudor domestic architecture is Dawn Court, 2A Lulworth Road, Birkdale, built as recently as 1934 for the managing director of Bear Brand hosiery. He engaged a London architect and builders from Deal to produce a true Tudor house using hand-made two-and-a-half-inch Tudor brick, hand-cut Cornish slate and oak floors and panelling.

It has everything in Tudor style from the characteristic steep-

*The walnut-panelled dining room of Rosefield Hall. [photo, Cyril Loker.]*

*Heavy, 'icing sugar' mouldings in a bedroom at Rosefield Hall. [photo, Cyril Loker.]*

*Every inch a Tudor house: Dawn Court, 2A Lulworth Road, Birkdale, built in 1934.*

pitched roof and tall, angular chimneys right down to such details as square downspouts and hopper heads. Every door and fireplace in the house has the characteristic Tudor arch—a late Perpendicular Gothic arch with a flattened point. Every room in the house is panelled—and furnished by the present owner, Mrs Alice Vyner-Brooks, with antique furniture dating from 1695.

There are other good examples of neo-Tudor half-timbering further along Lulworth Road and on Beach Road, Westbourne Road, Grosvenor Road, Lancaster Road, Waterloo Road and Selworthy Road in Birkdale, on Argyle Road, Cambridge Road, Rawlinson Road and Preston Road in the Hesketh Park district and on Scarisbrick New Road.

Chapter Thirteen

# *Ecclesiastical*

CHURCHES everywhere are generously documented by Arthur Mee and nearly every other travel and guide-book writer. Moreover, the churches of Southport are not generally outstanding, either architecturally or historically. There are some exceptions, architecturally, without mention of which this opus on Southport architecture would be incomplete.

By any standard the most magnificent church in Southport is Holy Trinity, on the corner of Hoghton Street and Manchester Road. This is Southport's 'cathedral' both in size and style, 200 ft. long, 66 ft. to the ridge of the nave, and its majestic buttressed and pinnacled tower rising 137 ft. high—the second tallest structure in Southport, after Blowick gas holder.

Inside, the cathedral effect is enhanced by the drama of Gothic arches soaring into lofty vaults, the dark lady chapel, the carved organ loft, the elaborate wood screen veiling the chancel, the ascent to the altar and the ethereal beauty of the reredos.

Not only is Holy Trinity like a cathedral, to those who have a feeling about buildings it bears a marked resemblance in style to Liverpool Cathedral, the mother church of the diocese. Built during 1903-14 to replace the earlier parish church of 1837, Holy Trinity was started just one year before the great cathedral on St. James's Mount. Like Giles Gilbert Scott at Liverpool, the architect of Holy Trinity, Huon Matear, who lived in Birkdale and practised in Liverpool, injected a new vitality into Gothic architecture. It was a new Gothic revival.

Both Liverpool Cathedral and Holy Trinity have the same feeling for vertical lines and the third dimension, the same sensuous feeling for the shape of red sandstone, the same awesome vastness and dim spaciousness—like a Wagnerian music drama in masonry, that all seems to come to life when resounding to the strains of the organ.

The projection of the third dimension on Holy Trinity is best seen on the west front as you approach it from the Law Courts. Observe the bold relief outlines and deep recesses of the tower, the great western window and the twin segmental-arch porches of the main entrance. The twin Gothic arches of the recessed west window are duplicated in separate arches, complete with tracery, standing out alone across the front of the recess.

The octagonal piers in the nave and the circular column in the north transept feature unusual natural markings in the red sandstone, which needs no further ornamentation. The piers of the nave have no capitals; their lines continue into the arches with but the merest suggestion of ornamentation in the simple recessed carvings, in place of capitals, which fade into the piers. There is a graceful network of ribbed vaulting in the chancel.

To me the most interesting carvings are those in the Lady Chapel. To look at the corbels around the base of the vaulting is to come face to face with the great leaders of the evangelisation of northern England in the seventh and eighth centuries A.D. (left to right): St. Paulinus, the first Archbishop of York; St. Bede, of Jarrow; St. Oswald, King of Northumbria; St. Hilda, Abbess of Whitby; St. Wilfred, Abbot of Ripon; and St. Aidan, Bishop of Lindisfarne. The wooden chancel screen, pulpit and organ loft are elaborately carved with grapevine, with snails on the leaves and birds pecking at the grapes.

*Southport's 'Cathedral': Holy Trinity Church.*
*[photo, Cedric Greenwood]*

The dramatic effects of the church are focussed on the reredos, a large carved wooden screen with four panels lined with a dark blue-based tapestry with a strangely transparent and luminous effect. At the centre is God the Father—his features just discernible at the centre of a cross of shafts of light, at his right is God the Son, at his left God the Holy Spirit, and underneath the personification of the seven gifts of God: charity, peace, sacrifice, mercy, hope, salvation and faith.

Like many other churches, Holy Trinity has reached the point where it has to be pulled down or restored owing to rainwater erosion and penetration of the fabric. Some of the stone tracery is in danger of falling out. To demolish this church would be unthinkable. The Historic Buildings and Monuments Commission rates Holy Trinity sufficiently important nationally to have made a massive £100,000 grant, 60 per cent of the £170,000 cost of the first phase of a five-year restoration, which will probably total £5 million. The church raised the balance and work was due to begin in January 1991.

***Right, top:*** *St. Marie's Church, Seabank Road.*
*[photo, Cedric Greenwood]*

Emmanuel Church (1895-98) on Cambridge Road is similarly spacious and elegant, again with octagonal piers and Gothic arches in red sandstone. The marble font is fascinating both for its markings and carving.

St. Cuthbert's (1730-39) in Churchtown is rather plain outside, being early Georgian, but the simple Georgian arch windows have been filled in with some trifling tracery. The inside, however, is a revelation.

***Right:*** *St. Joseph's Church, Birkdale.*
*[photo, Cedric Greenwood]*

Its beauty is, as it should be, mainly in the chancel with its classical Georgian arches and colonnaded screen. The chancel also features massive carved panels in heavy relief from the old St. Peter's Church that gave its name to Church Street, Liverpool. The Venetian window in the north wall was the original east window of 1730 but its rich stained glazing dates from about 1880.

The two Roman Catholic churches of St. Marie in Seabank Road and St. Joseph in Saxon Road are gems of Victorian Gothic Early English architecture on a modest scale by two eminent nineteenth-century Gothic exponents, Augustus and Edward Pugin, father and son, respectively. The two churches are similar in having a rose window on the west front, a Latin bellcote on the point of the gable and the organ loft above the west door.

A tablet inside St. Marie's tells us that mass was said occasionally in Southport from the beginning of the nineteenth century and there was a temporary chapel in Lord Street from 1827 to 1841, when the first church was built on this site in Seabank Road. Augustus Pugin's single-gable elevation without aisles was enlarged and rebuilt in 1852, 1875 and 1924 to the three-gable design with aisles and the broad Portland stone façade we see today.

Inside, quatrefoil columns (four columns in one) between the nave and the aisles support a clerestory roof with quatrefoil (four-leafed) windows along the clerestory. They lead to a five-sided apse with a painted ceiling and an alabaster altar with a fantastic three-dimensional form of Gothic tracery above.

The Emett bellcote on St. Joseph's Church stands above the tall, owl-haunted trees and Victorian villas of Birkdale Park. The buttressed red-brick walls with their tall, narrow, pointed windows, almost like arrow slits, give a stern appearance to this church by Edward Pugin, built in 1865-67, a single-gable elevation, enlarged with a south aisle lady chapel in 1875.

The inside of the church is a different story. Though less rich than St. Marie's in its decoration, St. Joseph's has a welcoming, restful interior, thanks to the softening of the

Gothic lines with a mansard ceiling, Romanesque vaulting in the apse and a very pleasant, rather cosy south aisle with its low ceiling, Tudor and segmental arch doorways off and the segmental arch west window embracing four trefoil-arch mullioned windows.

A stained glass rose window above the altar echoes the plain rose window above the west door. Other features are the octagonal pink sandstone columns between the nave and the south aisle and the inset panels around the walls of the nave with relief pictures in carved stone depicting the story of the crucifixion. They say a church is the house of God. St. Joseph's is the homeliest.

Two other ecclesiastical buildings, quite different in style, are also worthy of notice here. One is the old United Methodist Free Church in Duke Street, now the Masonic Hall. It was built in 1878-79, sturdy, foursquare and Italianate, with tall round-headed windows, a triangular pediment and an arcaded portico that bears a striking resemblance to the portico of the Arts Centre (1874)—both buildings had the same architects: Maxwell and Tuke, of Bury.

The other is the Scarisbrick family mausoleum in St. John's churchyard at Crossens. This small chapel, with coffins in the crypt, is a real little gem of Romanesque architecture, the only example of this style in Southport.

Its stocky gritstone walls accentuate the very modest windows with their vigorously carved semi-circular arches. At the east end a half-conical roof tops a semi-circular apse. There is a deep eaves line of arcaded corbels, carved with bird and animal heads. Zigzag carvings characteristically encircle the Romanesque door. The gable finials are robust wheel crosses.

*The former United Free Methodist Church, Duke Street, now the Masonic Hall. It was built in 1878-79 by the same architects as the Arts Centre—note the similar portico. The picture is taken from St. Paul's Square; note the derelict sewer-gas lamp on the right.*
*[photo, Cedric Greenwood]*

*The rugged little Romanesque mausoleum of the Scarisbrick family in St. John's churchyard at Crossens.*
*[photo,* Southport Visiter.*]*

The mausoleum was built in 1899-1901 by Ernest Johnson, who also designed the Albany Buildings and the Midland Bank in Lord Street. It belongs to the Trustees of the Scarisbrick Estates. Only twelve members of the Scarisbrick family have been interred there, the first in 1908, the last in 1967.

The weather has taken its toll on the fabric of the building and vandals broke into the chapel and vaults in the early 1970s, leaving evidence of Black Magic rites and the place had to be exorcised. A petition by St. John's Church to the Liverpool Diocesan Consistory Court to demolish the mausoleum was successfully opposed by the borough council and it is now a listed building and due for grant-aided restoration.

Chapter Fourteen

# George Tonge

PROBABLY the most important architect to practise in Southport and make his mark on the town was George Edward Tonge, FRIBA, FIAA, FRSA. He designed the town's largest and finest theatres and cinemas from 1911 to 1938, from the classical to the Art Deco.

Four of them are still with us: the Picture Palace, Lord Street (1911), now the Cannon cinema, the Bedford cinema, Bedford Road (1929), now a motor engineering workshop, the Garrick theatre, Lord Street (1932), now the Top Rank bingo club, and the Grand Cinema, Lord Street (1938), now the Grand casino and bingo club. He also designed the Royal Birkdale Golf Club (1936) in an open competition.

The Palladium, Lord Street (1913-14), later the Gaumont, then the Odeon, and the Palais de Danse (1925), later the Trocadero cinema (1929) were also his designs. They have been replaced by Sainsbury's and Woolworth's shops. Other cinema assignments were at Ainsdale, Seaforth, Litherland, Liverpool, Preston, Manchester, Oldham, Chester, Mold, Sleaford and Ilfracombe.

His life spanned the eighty years from 1876 to 1956, from the mid-Victorian period to the postwar period, times of great transition in architecture, and his own style changed with the times from the ornate late-Victorian to the plain 1930s modern.

Born at Over Hulton, he went to Bolton High School and Manchester School of Art, was articled to W. R. Howarth, a Bolton architect, in 1891 and was responsible for designing housing estates at Hulton Park and Westhoughton.

He came to Southport in 1900 to make up the partnership of Halsall, Tonge and Campbell in Lord Street between Christ Church and London Square and set up a practice on his own almost opposite, above the National Provincial Bank in 1927. In World War Two he was employed by the Ministry of Works on Ministry of Defence work with an office at Birkdale Palace Hotel. He finished his time at the Liverpool head office of Littlewood's department stores.

*George Tonge in 1935. [photo, courtesy of Maxwell Tonge]*

The Palace, Palladium and Palais de Danse were all classical in style. The Palace (Cannon) originally sported a central dome and corner cupolas but they were blacked out and eventually removed in

*The former Garrick Theatre (1932) on Lord Street. [photo, Cedric Greenwood]*

*The restored Art Deco interior of the Garrick Theatre, later the Essoldo Cinema, now the Top Rank Bingo Club. [photo, Cyril Loker.]*

recent modernisations. The detail above the canopy is Commercial Classic (such as we have seen in Chapter 8): oriel windows, portholes, mouldings and a wide Romanesque central arch. The Palladium and Palais bore a family resemblance with the Palace in style, rustication and mouldings but were more traditionally classical with colonnades and pilasters.

In the 1930s we see his transition with the vogue of the period to Art Deco in his Garrick Theatre and Royal Birkdale Golf Club and rebuilding of the Coliseum cinema in Nevill Street. The Garrick (Top Rank club) features a freestanding colonnade and the golf club house

looks like a 1930s' airport building. His later Grand cinema shows a return to a simplified classical style more akin to the Palace and the Palais.

*The Grand.*
*[photo, Cedric Greenwood]*

The Garrick Theatre, which became the Essoldo cinema in 1957, was held to be the finest theatre in Britain when it was built in 1932 and was the inspiration for a magnificent model, which George Tonge designed, of a 'dream theatre'. The proprietor of the Garrick, George Rose (whom we met at Rosefield Hall in Chapter 12) financed the construction of the model at a cost of £20,000 in 1935, and its exhibition tour of Britain by pantechnicon to raise funds for theatrical charities.

The model, in 5/8in:1ft scale, stood 14ft. square and 8ft. 6in. high and weighed three tons. More than 2,000 square feet of plywood and two and a half hundredweight of paint were used in the model. It was complete down to the 1,400 seats, scenery, refreshment rooms, dressing rooms, toilets, offices, kitchen appliances and working parts such as the revolving stage, lighting, heating and ventilation systems, all seen through glass partitions and observation panels in cutaway external walls. Internal walls were panelled in mahogany, walnut and grey walnut and even the pay boxes were fitted with working automatic ticket machines.

*Detail of George Tonge's Picture Palace (now the Cannon Cinema) of 1911.*
*[photo, Cedric Greenwood]*

George Tonge's diversions included cartooning and golf. He drew caricatures of well-known Southport personalities in the *Southport Graphic* in the Edwardian period and was captain of Southport Old Links Golf Club in 1914. After he retired he devoted himself to painting watercolour landscapes and portraits in oils. He lived at Hesketh Lodge, 138 Roe Lane, where his son, Mr Maxwell Tonge, who was also an architect, and daughter, Miss Joyce Tonge, still live. His other daughter, Mrs Gladys Grant, lives in Glasgow.

Mr Geoffrey Barnes of 319 Liverpool Road, Birkdale, recalls being an articled architect to George Tonge from leaving school at seventeen for the three years 1927-30. Apparently, George Tonge had an office above the shop that preceded the National Provincial Bank at the corner of Nevill Street and moved out for the construction of the bank in 1925-27.

He had a temporary office at 1 Hill Street when young Geoffrey joined him in 1927 and later that year occupied the top floor of the National Provincial Bank chambers, where in later years the architect Martin Perry had his office.

'George Tonge was a born artist and a genius,' says Mr Barnes. 'He had a very genial and likeable temperament. He was quite a gentleman.'

Mr Barnes worked with George Tonge on the design of the Plaza cinema and ballroom (on the site of the Natterjack Restaurant) at Ainsdale in 1927, the Bedford cinema in Birkdale in 1929, the conversion of the Palais de Danse to the Trocadero cinema in 1930 and the enlargement of the Picture Palace also in 1930. The Palace was originally a single-storey building and the roof of the auditorium behind the dome and cupolas was jacked up 17 feet 6 inches, the walls being built up as it was lifted, to accommodate a balcony. Mr Barnes recalls that the operation was completed without so much as a crack appearing in the plaster ceiling. Mr Barnes was later assistant architect in the borough engineer's department at Southport (1947-49) and public health inspector at Bootle (1955-72).

Mr Barnes, who is now eighty, is the author of the *Birkdale Historic Trail*, published by Birkdale Civic Society. He became interested in the history of rural Birkdale (before 1850) when he first visited the oil-lit thatched cottage at 74 Liverpool Road in the 1940s. He was instrumental in getting the cottage spot-listed when it was threatened with redevelopment.

Chapter Fifteen

# London Square

ALMOST every town and city in England is gathered around its market cross, its clock tower, its fountain, its petrified Queen Victoria, its corporation geranium beds or, simply, a roundabout. Does any town or city in Britain have such a splendid centrepiece as a focal point as Southport's Monument in London Square? Does any town or city have such a noble and poignant monument to its war-slain than this white Portland stone obelisk, colonnades and water gardens? What more suitable site for a great monument than this central point for all to see, flanked by gardens and trees? The tower of Christ Church and the spire of St. George's add to the dramatic symmetry.

The Monument was built in 1923 and unveiled by the Earl of Derby

*The Monument, London Square.*
*[photo, Cedric Greenwood]*

on Remembrance Day of that year. Before 1923, London Square was just a wide open space, paved with wood blocks, between the Lord Street gardens with a hackney carriage drivers' hut and a public lavatory in the middle of it.

London Square is so named because it is at the downtown end of London Street, which formerly led to the hamlet of Little London, now marked by the London Hotel at Kensington Road/Windsor Road crossing and the Blue Anchor in Tithebarn Road.

It took a war to transform the square into a fitting centre for our beautiful town. The townspeople subscribed to it as an equally fitting monument to the 1,133 Southport soldiers and sailors who died in World War One—well over ten per cent of the volunteers from Southport.

The magnitude and success of the war memorial are largely due to the fact that the appeal to the public interest and sentiment were made at a time when the public heart and conscience were touched and the mood of thanksgiving and remembrance was still strong. Three months after Victory Day, a public meeting decided to raise a fund to build a monument, to give Victory Scholarships to assist the education of the children of Southport soldiers and sailors who died in the war and to give the residue of the fund to an extension of the Infirmary. The appeal raised £31,850 which would be worth at least £2,000,000 today!

The design of the monument was put out to open competition. Forty-five designs were submitted from architects all over the country,

*The water gardens, colonnades and obelisk all go to make up The Monument, Southport's tribute to its 1,133 volunteers who died in World War One. [photo,* Southport Visiter.*]*

*Looking through the coupled Renaissance Doric columns of the east colonnade to the Greek Ionic columns that guard the sanctum of the cenotaph at the northern end.*
*[photo,* Southport Visiter.*]*

including Southport, and the adjudicator, Sir Reginald Blomfield, a famous London architect, picked the design by the firm of Grayson and Barnish, of the Royal Liver Building, Liverpool.

Three architects worked on the scheme: Hastewell Grayson, Leonard Barnish, formerly of Southport, and A. L. McMillan, of Southport. They decided that the narrowness of London Street and the volume of traffic—even then—demanded a feature of great height on a confined base. The model for the obelisk was cast and re-cast many times to get the proportions of the shaft, base and plinth quite satisfactory. The obelisk as built stands 67ft. 6in. tall.

The obelisk and the square are flanked by twin colonnades with coupled Doric columns and coffered ceilings, Greek Ionic columns guard the entrances, inside the colonnades, to the cenotaphs—the temples or sanctums at the ends of the colonnades in which the names of Southport's 1,133 dead are inscribed on marble tablets.

Yes, these are the cenotaphs, and it is in these four chambers—two in each colonnade—out of the wind and rain, where the wreaths should be laid on Remembrance Day, not at the foot of the obelisk.

After the Liverpool architects came the Liverpool sculptor, H. Tyson Smith, who did the bas-relief carvings and the inscriptions.

Simplicity, purity and quiet strength is the keynote of the design of The Monument and decorative carving has been kept to the minimum. However, there is considerably more than most people notice in passing and the most notable are the bas-relief carvings of Britannia on the outer walls of the cenotaphs facing Lord Street.

The one on the north colonnade shows Britannia, with a sword hanging from her right wrist, holding a statuette of Victory aloft in her left hand. On the south colonnade Britannia pays tribute to the dead, represented by a military helmet.

The main inscriptions are in elegant letters 1 ft. tall along the friezes of the colonnades: 'Tell Britain, ye who mark this monument; faithful to her we fell and rest content,' 'To all famous men all Earth is sepulchre' and 'Their portion is with the eternal.' The wording of these inscriptions is as poignant as the architecture of The Monument itself.

The globular lamps around the colonnades and the water gardens with their fountains are all part of The Monument.

By great good fortune this monumental composition is fittingly complemented by four equally megalithic classical buildings that are the four cornerstones of London Square: the National Westminster Bank, Russell & Bromley's shoe shop, the former National Provincial Bank and Lloyd's Bank.

Which is the odd one out? Russell & Bromley's you might say, because all the others were built as banks. Architecturally the odd one out is the National Westminster Bank because this, the only one of the four that was built before The Monument (in 1892), is in yellow sandstone and is very much an original piece of Victorian free-style classical architecture without columns, whereas the other three buildings are, like The Monument itself, all in white Portland stone and feature classical orders. Russell & Bromley's (originally Alexander's fashion store) was built in the same year as The Monument (1923) and rose to the occasion with engaged Ionic columns, pilasters and Roman arches, although there is too much glass in the facade for the building to be listed as an example of classical architecture.

The National Provincial Bank and Lloyd's Bank followed in 1925-27 and 1927-28 respectively and within the span of six years London Square had been transformed into a superlatively noble and handsome town centre, fit for the capital city whose name it bears.

If we were asked which structure was the representative hallmark of Southport—like Liverpool's Liver Building, Chester's East Gate, York's Minster and Newcastle's Tyne Bridge—I think we should all say The Monument. We grow up from childhood to look upon it as a symbol of security and serenity—of Southport's golden age.

Chapter Sixteen

# *Birkdale*

A TERRITORIAL name eight hundred years before Southport, Birkdale (Old Norse 'birk-dal', birch valley), was still, in the late 1840s, a bosky defile in the windswept coastal sandhills with scattered farms, thatched cottages and a post mill on the heys, or meadows, between the sandhills and the inland moss, when just over the manorial boundary Southport had grown into a fashionable town.

They still call the centre of Birkdale a 'village' today but this is a misnomer. This street of shops is not a village and never was. Up to 1850 there was no building between the railway and the thatched cottage at 74 Liverpool Road. Birkdale village was three-quarters of a mile south along Liverpool Road.

The centre of old Birkdale and the village green were at what is now Liverpool Road Methodist Church on the corner of Sandon Road. The first Birkdale railway station, built in 1848, was at the nearest point to this on the railway, between Dunkirk Road and Sheringham Road.

Now accounting for what may be 20,000 of Southport's 90,000 population, Birkdale is no village. It is a town in its own right. Back in 1863 the Birkdale Board of Local Commissioners was formed. Birkdale had its own town hall in 1871, its own police station in 1891, its own fire station in 1900 and its own Carnegie Library in 1904, all together in a kind of civic centre on Weld Road south of York Road crossing. Birkdale Urban District Council was formed in 1894, Ainsdale was annexed to the urban district in 1905 and Birkdale remained independent—like Hove to Brighton—until amalgamation with Southport in 1912.

The town hall, library and police station were demolished in 1971 but there are still other remnants of Birkdale's separate entity: the invisible straight line across the town map like a geological fault, where straight roads bend and side streets end in cul-de-sacs, and manhole covers marked 'B.L.B.' (Birkdale Local Board) and 'B.D.C.' (Birkdale District Council).

The hedge that divides the bowling green from the rest of Victoria Park is the boundary between Southport and Birkdale and that divide can be seen on Rotten Row: on the Southport side the houses front on to Rotten Row but on the Birkdale side they back on to it with their back gardens atop the bank.

Despite Birkdale's independent development it grew up along the same lines as its fashionable 'garden city' neighbour, with large villas along quiet, tree-shaded streets—not straight and level like Southport's but gracefully curving and gently rising and falling.

The development of Birkdale Park (described under Victorian Villas) began in 1850 and high-class 'marine residences' were built in the sandhills seaward of the railway from the Southport boundary. Thus Aughton Road, York Road, Gloucester Road, Lulworth Road, Westcliffe Road and Weld Road appeared on the map.

Where Liverpool Road from old Birkdale met Weld Road on the corner of Birkdale Park a new railway station was built (on the present site) in 1851 and this became the centre of the new township, with the town hall etc. on one side of the railway and the main street of shops on the other.

As the train slides out of the Victorian suburban station across the main street of Birkdale, there is a brief image of an Edwardian small town centre with a main street of noble banks, colonnaded shops and wide sidewalks framed and shaded by trees.

This is a picture most people would not like to change. In 1971 it did change. The centrepiece of this view, a group of shops at the corner of Liverpool Road and Alma Road, was demolished and rebuilt in yellow-brick lavatory-block style.

If the whole main street of Birkdale were rebuilt in this austere modern style, the image, the character and the pleasure of shopping there would be lost. It would look like a shopping parade anywhere. Hence the designation of the Birkdale Conservation Area in 1981.

Fortunately, the key building in the main street scene looking north is the Barclay's Bank (late Martin's Bank), which is the most distinguished and interesting building in the street. Built in 1907 as the

*Birkdale main street, looking north, showing Victoria Chambers (left) and Barclays Bank (right). [photo, Cedric Greenwood]*

*Barclay's Bank (late Martin's Bank), Birkdale, built in 1907. [photo,* Southport Visiter.*]*

Bank of Liverpool, it features a beautiful semi-elliptical stone arch doorway framed by pilasters supporting a gracefully curved stone pediment, stone mullioned and bowed windows—one of the bow windows nicely rounding off the corner of the building—and ornate scroll gables capped with curved pediments.

The former District Bank on the corner of Abbey Gardens is the second most prominent feature in the main street with its green copper cupola and contrasting white Portland stonework and red Accrington brickwork. This was another casualty of the National Westminster Bank amalgamations and has lost something in the conversion to shops. Like Barclay's Bank, it has a rounded corner, under the cupola, with curved stonework and curved glazing. This bank was built in 1911 as the Manchester and County Bank and the initials 'M. C.' are carved in a stone frieze on the corner and the monogram 'M & CBLd' frosted in the glazing.

*Pure and simple classical good looks: the Midland Bank, Birkdale, built in 1908.*
*[photo,* Southport Visiter.*]*

*The Royal Bank of Scotland (late William Deacon's Bank), Birkdale, built in 1894.*
*[photo,* Southport Visiter.*]*

The inconspicuous Midland Bank, a single-storey building in the shade of the trees, is perhaps the most beautiful piece of architecture in Birkdale's main street. It is a model of simple classical good looks and smartness in red brick and white Portland stone; three Roman arch windows flanked by stone-capped piers, a square-headed doorway with pilasters supporting a triangular pediment, magnificent panelled oak doors, a balustraded parapet and a rusticated stone plinth. It was built in 1908.

The Royal Bank of Scotland (late William and Glyn's Bank, formerly Williams Deacon's Bank) is the oldest bank in Birkdale, built in 1894. It is a fairly simple suburban exercise in Victorian Commercial Classic (described in Lord Street Medley) and is notable for its curved and carved pilasters, or extended trusses, supporting the lintel over the door, for its Romanesque door and windows on the ground floor frontage, its moulded friezes above the first floor windows and the oval window and moulding in the gable.

Completing a very fine collection of banks in this short section of street is the four-storey Queen Anne-style National Westminster (late Westminster) Bank, so easily missed behind the trees and street furniture on the shady side of the street. It was built in 1911 and the Queen Anne features are the Romanesque arches in the rusticated stonework on the ground floor, the thick glazing bars and proportions of the windows set in the red brick elevation of the first and second floors, the prominent cornice with dentils and the fourth-floor dormer windows. Note the carved woodwork of the arched windows.

*Neo-Queen Anne: the National Westminster Bank (late Westminster Bank, 1911. [photo, Cedric Greenwood]*

Dominating the main street on the point of the bend are Victoria Chambers, terminating the view from Alma Road. The date on a hopperhead is 1894 and above the glazed iron colonnade are oriel windows and red sandstone carvings and plaster mouldings in the gables. It is worrying that these upper stories are empty and not let as offices or flats because the fabric looks neglected.

Rounding the bend from the south the street scene is terminated by the long, weatherboard railway signal cabin with its myriad small windows, set at right angles to the street. Not only does it contribute to the townscape but it half closes off Liverpool Road from Weld Road. There would be a wide open gap in the townscape in the centre of Birkdale if the cabin were to be removed in the centralisation of signal and gate functions scheduled for 1991.

Some of Birkdale's great wealth and range of domestic architecture has already been featured: the thatched cottage at 74 Liverpool Road, the Regency-Gothick villas at 43-47 Aughton Road, 6 Lulworth Road and 3 Westcliffe Road, the Victorian villas at 1 Lulworth Road, 2, 6, 13 and 26 Westcliffe Road, 3 and 5 Grosvenor Road, 23 Gloucester Road and 12-14 York Road and the neo-Tudor house at 2A Lulworth Road.

Chapter Seventeen

# *The Round House*

AN observatory? A coastguard station? A lighthouse? The Round House at 61 Waterloo Road, Birkdale, has been a source of interest and speculation as to what it was and why it was built circular.

It was built in 1924-25 as a private residence and is circular simply because the builder, Luke Highton, of Southport, had always wanted to build a rotunda. He built it with a red brick plinth and brick banding (now covered with roughcast) and a 14ft. diameter glass dome on the flat roof as an . . . observatory.

He realised his ambition late in life. He was 74 when he built it and lived there seven years until he died at 81. Before he died, Luke Highton was host at The Round House to a party of members of the British Astronomical Association, who came to watch the moon's

*The Round House, 61 Waterloo Road, Birkdale. [photo, Cedric Greenwood]*

***Left:** The entrance hall to the Round House is finished in Wedgwood green and white. [photo, Cyril Loker.]*

***Below:** A segment of the circular walls can be seen in this picture of part of the long, curving lounge, which looks out over the sandhills to the sea. [photo, Cyril Loker.]*

eclipse of the sun in 1927. Southport was right in the path of that eclipse and The Round House was an ideal place for observing it.

The house is built on the highest point in town and from the top is an uninterrupted 360-degree panorama of mountains, plains, sand-hills, sea and sky from the Cambrian mountains in the south to the Cumbrian mountains in the north.

The former owner of the house, the late Mr L. Bowen, did not have a telescope but with a powerful pair of 20x120 binoculars (reputed to be from a Japanese warship) could pick out a slim television mast on the Denbighshire moors and Blackpool tramcars at Starr Gate and read the time on the Liver clock, which filled the lens. He could even follow golf balls to the farthest green on the Royal Birkdale golf links. 'As an incurable golf addict this suits me great,' said Mr Bowen.

He bought The Round House in 1962. 'It was all corridors and tiny rooms,' he said. So in 1963 he commissioned Preston and Norris Ltd. of Waterloo to remodel the interior and they made extensive—and tasteful—alterations.

The showpiece of the house is the hall with its white pilasters and arches set in Wedgwood green walls and its white panelled ceiling. The beauty of the house is the irregular shape of every room, fitted in between the circular walls, the hall, stairs and landings.

On the second floor, at the top of the house, is the observation lounge facing the sea, a bedroom and two sun balconies. The front door is in the north side of the house but faces west in a circular porch with tall slit windows. The porch was added by Preston and Norris to shield the blast of the prevailing wind in this open spot when you open the house door.

The long, curving lounge has ten windows and two 'portholes' looking out over the golf links and the grass covered sandhills to the sea and, of an evening, the room is lit by beautiful and savage sunsets over the western horizon. In this elevated position with a 360-degree scan, one is made very sensitive to the weather and the changing seasons.

The Round House is now home to the Holmes family, who have restored the original style of windows to the front of the house, copying them from those left at the back of the house. They also hope to restore the glass dome on the roof, not for astronomy but simply for the look of it. Mr Robert Holmes told me: 'What threw me at first was that I did not know which way I was facing. There seems to be no sense of direction in the house. I had to look out of the window to see which way I was facing.'

Chapter Eighteen

# *Domestic revivals*

DESPITE the modern movement in architecture from the 1930s to the 1970s, seen in offices, shops, factories and schools, houses went on being built in traditional styles. When it came to choosing a place to live, people were not attracted by concrete and glass, flat roofs and metal windows. A few homes were built in the modern idiom but by far the majority continued to be derivatives of the Tudor house.

The more discerning customers—and those who could afford custom-built houses—opted for classical designs. Classicism in commercial and public buildings ended with World War Two but since the war there has been something of a revival of the domestic architecture of the classical era.

I do not refer to houses with bow windows and pediments on pillars for porticos that pass for 'Georgian' houses. We are in danger of forgetting what a Georgian house really is. Applied details do not make a Georgian house.

The essence of classical architecture is its monumental simplicity and good proportions. More than any other style of architecture it relies on good design rather than ornamentation for its effect. In the mid-twentieth-century trend towards economy and the functional, many house builders have turned back to classical architecture for sheer foursquare, honest simplicity and good looks. You can build a box to classical rules and it looks good.

There is an isolated 'seam' of neo-Classical houses along Selworthy Road, Birkdale, and on the intersecting stretch of Waterloo Road. Although there are no serious replicas of particular styles of the classical era, the architects have obviously invoked the style and spirit of the era or at least some classical features to produce some really good looking modern houses.

Mr Ernest Ball, a Southport architect, designed and built for himself The Pantiles at 1 Selworthy Road in 1927. It has an Italianate flavour engendered by the pantiled roof, the prominent overhang of the eaves, the semi-circular arches over the ground floor windows and the arcaded porch with Tuscan stone columns. The two-storey bow is characteristic late-Georgian.

*Neo-Queen Anne: Merry Hill, 24 Selworthy Road, Birkdale, built in 1955. [photo,* Southport Visiter.*]*

Merry Hill, no. 24 Selworthy Road, is a Queen Anne house, the only Queen Anne house in Southport: bold and rectangular with a parapet, a hipped roof and a tall chimney at the side. The ivy covering adds a rustic touch to the period charm. It was built in 1955.

There are several neo-Georgian houses on Selworthy Road—or rather pseudo-Georgian, usually featuring beautiful white panelled, pilastered and pedimented front doors and some round-headed windows but otherwise paying only lip service to Georgian architecture.

The characteristic Georgian house is the terrace house, flat-fronted with a minimum of detail but with beautiful proportions of apertures to wallspace. The bow windows invoked by modern 'Georgian' house builders featured only on Georgian shops to display the goods. The bijou neo-Georgian houses in Wellington Street are therefore not typical of what they represent but they have a Georgian feeling and character both outside and in, which sets them in a class apart from other neo-Georgian houses of today.

One side of the street—five units out of eight anyway—has been transfigured by a man of vision, Mr David Glover, a Lord Street antique furnisher, who bought and converted the houses as they came on the market. His ideas were put down in two dimensions by Southport architect Mr James Orwell and put up in three dimensions by local builder, Mr James McGuinness.

The transformation is not confined to the façades but is carried right through to the backs of the houses, making gracious homes for those fortunate enough to live there. Mr Glover hopes to be able to convert

*Wellington Street as it was before.*
*[photo, David Glover.]*

*And as it appeared in 1989.*
*[photo, Cedric Greenwood]*

the whole block in due course.

Glebe House was remodelled in 1969 from an existing house, 13 Wellington Street, built in 1837, and is now Mr Glover's home. Friends told Mr Glover he was mad when be bought the small, nondescript terrace house at no. 13—but he had observed the pediment.

That pediment was the catalyst of the Georgianisation not only of no. 13 but of all the others that followed. Mr Glover could see the potential; he had the imagination to visualise the house we see today. Vision is half the battle in improving a house but, instead of modernising it as people usually do, he made it more old-fashioned.

***Right:*** *A brand new Georgian house: Nile Court, 1-3 Wellington Street, replaced two shops in 1970-71.*
*[photo,* Southport Visiter.*]*

***Below:*** *Glebe House, 13 Wellington Street, remodelled from an ordinary terrace house in 1969.*
*[photo, Cedric Greenwood]*

He turned the clock back to the Georgian period; with a pediment like that, what else could he do?

He had to go a long way—to Hertfordshire, in fact, to find a joiner who would make him the barrelled windows and the semi-circular canopy over the front door. The barrel windows are roofed in curving fans of lead. White shutters were fitted to the first floor windows. The pediment was re-capped with a Georgian cornice.

The bull's-eye panes in the barrel windows look down on a cobbled forecourt enclosed by tall iron railings and gates. The gate piers are topped by carved stone pineapples.

By night the house takes on a new enchantment. When the lights go up, those barrel windows give the passer-by a vision of gracious Georgian living. It's like looking in the window of a period house in a folk museum—but somebody really lives here. As an antique dealer Mr Glover has been able to furnish his house suitably with elegant furniture of the eighteenth and early nineteenth centuries and the rooms provide the perfect setting for his own collection of antique ornaments.

The coach-yellow front door opens straight into a transverse lounge-dining

*The lounge of Glebe House, showing the carved wooden fire surround and alcoves, the carved 17th-century spiral columns and some of the 18th- and 19th-century furnishings. [photo, Cyril Loker.]*

room, which was made out of the two small front rooms and the central corridor by inserting steel girders across the ceiling. The main features of this room are the carved pine fireplace and alcoves and the twin spiral pillars, carved out of tree trunks, with grapevines and birds in relief. The pillars are believed to be 17th-century and Mr Glover found them in Florence. In the original conversion of the house, two white Renaissance Corinthian plaster pillars stood here, ostensibly supporting the ceiling between the lounge and dining sections.

The rest of the house has also been extensively redesigned and rebuilt and there is even a large bow window at the back to give more light and space to the landing. All the cornices in the house are cast from eighteenth century moulds.

Nile Court is a completely new house, built in 1970-71 on the site of two former shops at 1 and 3 Wellington Street. It is a double-fronted house divided into three apartments with one front door, flanked by fluted pilasters and two bow windows. Above the door is a fanlight with interlaced arches and a semicircular canopy that is also a balcony. A low wall and iron railings enclose a cobbled forecourt.

Inside, all the carved pine fireplaces have different motifs and different coloured marble surrounds: green marble in the vestibule, blue and soft lilac marble in the blue apartment, soft grey marble in the white apartment and gold marble in the gold apartment. Again the cornices are made from eighteenth century moulds.

In 1973, Mr Glover converted nos. 9 and 11 Wellington Street. A Renaissance Ionic portico frames the twin front doors and the two houses are identical inside, the one being a mirror of the other.

The wall between the entrance hall and the lounge has been

replaced with a glazed partition with no door, welcoming you into the lounge and virtually merging the hall and lounge into one, giving a greater feeling of space.

A partition with an arched window blocks the through passage from the hall to the stairs, which now make a right-angled turn into the dining room. The front and back rooms have become a through lounge-diner with carved pine fireplaces and alcoves.

Renaissance Ionic pillars flank the way between the lounge and dining sections and the fore-and-aft room gives a view through the French doors of an illuminated patio rock garden and waterfall, enclosed by 9ft. high walls.

Finally, we come to one of Southport's newest houses, built in 1987-89 in a style that harks back to Elizabethan—not timber-framed but brick-and-stone Elizabethan: 26A Lulworth Road, Birkdale.

Birkdale builder Mr Bill Wharton did not consciously build an Elizabethan house when he built himself a home in between building others but he and his wife, Carole, who drafted the design, knew what they liked. Among the buildings they liked was Carr House, Bretherton, which this house resembles.

Mr Wharton got the old brick from a demolished mill at Rochdale. The hood mouldings over the windows are in reconstituted stone. There are no Elizabethan features inside but there is plenty of good solid woodwork, a second-hand oak fireplace, cast-iron radiators and a porcelain kitchen sink.

This modest essay in neo-Elizabethan brickwork and its ostentatious modern next-door neighbour were built on the site of the former St. James's vicarage, which was the only red sandstone house in Southport and a very fine house too. It was a casualty of the Church Commissioners' policy of disposing of large vicarages.

*Neo-Elizabethan: 26A Lulworth Road, Birkdale. [photo, Cedric Greenwood]*

# *Epilogue*

THE finishing touches to the Lord Street scene were The Monument in 1923, the District Bank in 1924 and the National Provincial Bank in 1927. That was the golden age of Southport architecture. The Garrick Theatre was added in 1932, ushering in the new modernism, and the Grand cinema in 1938.

Southport saw little change in the physical fabric of the townscape in the 1930s, '40s and '50s and the town was lucky to escape the 'comprehensive redevelopment' that gutted and transfigured so many town centres in the 1960s and '70s with bleak blocks of concrete and glass—offices, shopping 'precincts' and flats—in an anonymous, universal idiom so that you could not tell if you were in Swindon or Swinton, Vancouver or Vladivostock.

While it escaped comprehensive redevelopment, Southport did not entirely escape the Philistinism of the 1960s and '70s, matched by the mentality in planning circles that let anything go. Brash brutalism came to Chapel Street in a big slab of mosaic-sheeted concrete that reached right from Marks & Spencer to the station car park in London Street in 1970 to replace the Lancashire & Yorkshire Railway terminus. The curtailed railway is reached through a dingy, draughty tunnel of shuttered shops like a scene for a mugging on the New York subway—the very antithesis of a welcome for arrivals to a gracious Victorian floral resort.

The year 1970, indeed, was the year it all happened; it was the worst year of modernist developments that disfigured the town—developments that are now regarded as mistakes. There was not only the station shopping 'precinct' but also the cubist concrete 'cascade' that masks the Arts Centre, the Blackpool 'golden mile' buildings that disguise the pier entrance and the ugly nine-storey yellow-brick block of flats on the site of the former Victoria Hotel on the promenade at the top of Nevill Street.

The same austerity crept into our domestic environment with brick cubes of flats nestling among the Victorian villas of Hesketh Park and Birkdale Park. It was a time of architectural blight, when buildings were thrown up in their most elementary form, completely devoid of imagination and character.

The same Philistinism was reflected in the neglect and decay of Lord Street—its buildings, iron colonnades, gardens and street

*The Philistine period: bleak walls imprison the junction of Chapel Street and Eastbank Street.*
*[photo,* Southport Visiter.*]*

furniture. In fact, when I first mooted a conservation area for Southport in 1970, the official view was that there was nothing in Southport worth conserving, except, perhaps, the iron colonnades! The future looked bleak. There was no respect for old buildings and no awareness of the importance of the environment to human beings.

The scene has changed radically since the first edition of this book was published in 1971. It made people aware of their environment, it made them look up above the shop canopies. Above all, it inspired the next chairman of the borough planning committee, the late Cllr. Tony Daniels, to moot the Lord Street conservation area that was designated in January 1973.

Slowly, in the mid-1970s, the Philistine movement was reversed by the new conservation movement. More conservation areas were designated and then came conservation architecture—the brave new world of 1980s' brickwork with pitched roofs, hips and gables, curves and arches, oriel windows, brick and stone banding and stone quoins and architraves. The best examples in Southport are Sainsbury's grocery supermarket (1982) and Percival Court flats (1988), both in Lord Street.

Conservation areas were designated in Churchtown (Botanic Road) in November, 1973, Birkdale (main street from Welbeck Road to York Road) in October, 1981, and West Birkdale (Westbourne Road and parts of Grosvenor Road and Lancaster Road) in November, 1988. Churchtown conservation area was extended to Manor Road and Little Cambridge Road in April, 1989, and the borough conservation officer, Mr Graham Arnold, is currently working on a conservation area for The Promenade, which was due to be designated in December 1990. Designation by itself is only half the battle. It is a declaration of intent by the borough council to carry out works and only to allow development that will preserve and enhance the character of the townscape. It requires conservation area consent to demolish any part of a building but not for normally permitted alterations and extensions. The borough conservation officer has to persuade property owners and tenants on repair leases of the wisdom of the repair and maintenance of their buildings.

The Historic Buildings and Monuments Commission and the borough council can make discretionary twenty-five per cent grants towards eligible repairs. The 1979 Town Scheme, offering combined fifty per cent (now forty per cent) grants from the HBMC and the borough council has persuaded many owners and tenants to part with fifty per cent (now sixty per cent) of the cost of structural repair and restoration of the external fabric and the iron colonnades on eligible buildings in Lord Street.

Persuasion was an uphill battle at first but, once a few had made the improvement, the restoration movement began to snowball through Lord Street in the 1980s. The former borough conservation officer (1975-87), Mr Michael King, said: 'Once the philosophy of repair began, the market began to demand to do it, as opposed to a negative attitude.'

In my first edition, I advocated a conservation area stretching from Manchester Road (Arnside Road) to Liverpool Road (Welbeck Road), taking in Lord Street, Hoghton Street, The Promenade and Birkdale Park. Bit by bit we have almost achieved that. What is missing is conservation protection for the Regency and Regency Gothick houses at the lower end of Manchester Road, the many fine Italianate houses and offices along Hoghton Street and the Victorian villas of Birkdale Park, notably in Westcliffe Road, Aughton Road, York Road,

*One of the many fine Italianate buildings in Hoghton Street: Nos. 22-24. [photo, Cedric Greenwood]*

Gloucester Road and Saxon Road. Many of these buildings may be borderline cases or just under par for listing but as groups they form a townscape worth conserving.

It is almost too late to conserve Birkdale Park—almost, but not quite. Had it been done along with Lord Street in 1973, together with the link through Lord Street West, it would have regulated the overpowering blocks of flats that have continued to muscle-in among the family homes and the disappearance of gardens under car parks, garages and cul-de-sacs of mean brick huts.

This kind of development tends to have a knock-on effect: as the builders move in the neighbours move out and the builders move in next door and so it goes on along the street. The north-east end of Birkdale Park is overripe for conservation to protect the still considerable number of fine family houses and gardens, the amenities of the residents, the quiet, bosky streets, the wildlife and the natural drainage of the area from further incursions of slate and tarmac of purely speculative development.

Conversion to rest homes and nursing homes has saved many a large Victorian villa from decay and redevelopment. They were looking dowdy in 1971 but have now been attractively restored and given a new lease of life.

Southport was lucky to survive the redevelopment craze of the 1960s. It will not survive the even greater redevelopment era now upon us but this seems likely to improve the town rather than detract.

There are good examples of 1980s' brickwork and imaginative conservation architecture in Jim Moon's designs for the Jones Retirement Homes, Maplewood (1986) in Cambridge Road and Percival Court (1988) in Lord Street. Both are lively compositions of pitched and hipped roofs and gables with modest windows and string courses of different brick or stone. Maplewood has a varied roof line

*Maplewood, Cambridge Road: a good example of '1980s' brickwork, designed, like Percival Court by Jim Moon for Jones Retirement Homes. [photo, Cedric Greenwood]*

and building line and variegated brickwork. Percival Court features inverted arches and stone balustrading in the surrounding brick wall to echo the arched stone tympanums above the ground floor windows and the balustrading around the Lord Street gardens. Percival Court is a great improvement on the former ABC cinema, which it replaced, and even puts the neighbouring prestige block, Viceroy Court, to shame, although that has since had a facelift, which has further improved the scene.

New shopping schemes like Cambridge Walks (1988-89) and Marble Place (1989-90) are a definite improvement on the 'Sally Anne' desert behind the 'Queen Anne' façade of Lord Street and there was even a scheme to demolish the station shopping block in Chapel Street and London Street only twenty years after it was built and remodel it with red-brick gables and oriel windows on the existing frame-work and realign and extend the arcade to replace that nasty tunnel.

*Percival Court, which replaced the ABC Cinema at the corner of Lord Street and Wellington Street in 1988. [photo, Lighthouse Studios, Knutsford.]*

The Winter Gardens shopping centre bids to restore Lord Street station with its noble clock tower and put back the glass canopy over the forecourt. The design for a multi-storey car park like a Moorish fort on the Esplanade should rank for an award for a solution to the vexed problem of encasing multi-storey parking and add a touch of light fantasy to the sea front. Seaside fantasy was lost with the demolition of the Pier Pavilion and the destruction by fire of the Colonnade in Prince's Park and the gate towers of Pleasureland.

The Winter Gardens scheme has the right architectural approach but seems too grandiose in scale. There must be a limit to Southport's capacity for shops and restaurants and I should hate it to become a 'white elephant' or to kill the trade at the other end of Lord Street. Neither am I keen on the idea of a department store on the sea front but both this and the scale of the development might be acceptable if the planners pursue a policy of land reclamation and expansion of the town centre to seaward with a new sea front to meet the distant sea.

With almost all the building land in the borough used up and the sea a thin grey line on the horizon, if nature is inclined to build up the coastline with sand, spartina grass and dunes, we should not fight it but go with nature and use the opportunity to expand the town to seaward over the rather scruffy seafront desert and shantyville we have now and lay out a much more attractive sea front where the sea is an ever-present attraction.

These are exciting times in Southport but it all needs coordination and strong guidance from planners of imagination and vision who know what they want and are prepared to give leadership in planning and conservation to be one jump ahead of all the pressures of population, traffic and commercial interests that are exerted on the town today. Certainly Southport is in much better circumstances today than it was at the time of the first edition of this book eighteen years ago. The fabric of the town is in a better condition, the place is generally more attractive and the prospects for the future are brighter, thanks to a greater public awareness and appreciation of our heritage.

There were no contributions to the Lord Street scene from the 1920s until the 1980s, when Martin Perry's Victorian-style bandstand and information pavilion were added. It is difficult to enhance a townscape like Lord Street and so easy to detract from it. Mr Perry is also the

*The tourist information pavilion in Eastbank Street, by Martin Perry, 1988. [photo, Cedric Greenwood]*

architect of much restoration on Lord Street and secretary of the Southport Civic Society. I shall let him sum up the state of the three-dimensional art in the town he so loves and to which he has probably contributed more, architecturally, than any other living person.

He writes: 'Since the first edition of Cedric Greenwood's book in 1971, have we made steps forward in the conservation of Southport and what of the future'?

'Lord Street was made a conservation area in 1973 and this has had a dramatic effect on building repairs and in particular on shopping canopy repairs, where grants are now available. The private shop-keepers have been quicker to react to the conservation area than some of the multiple companies and there are still several Lord Street buildings and canopies in disrepair.

'Lord Street contains several major public buildings and the council renovated the white stucco Town Hall in 1980 and Crown and Bank Building on the corner of Eastbank Street in 1989—the latter having the original rooftop balustrading replaced. The intervening Atkinson Library and Art Gallery and Cambridge Hall buildings have had substantial internal renovations but need urgent external restoration to save deteriorating stonework.

'Lord Street gardens and street design have improved to a degree but long awaited garden restoration work throughout the length of Lord Street, including substantial refurbishment of the central gardens, do not appear to have attracted sufficient political attention to enable work to be done in an appropriate manner or general maintenance to be properly carried out.

'Major town centre shopping developments are newly completed or underway. These have been more carefully detailed than their counterparts of the 1960s and less destructive to the street character. However, the effect on traffic and on increased shopping space in

Southport has yet to be seen.

'One other major trend over the last ten years is the enormous growth in rest homes and nursing homes, usually formed by converting large, older residential property. Southport has a wealth of gracious Edwardian and Victorian houses and villas. Rest homes have successfully generated funds to maintain and convert these buildings against the frequent alternatives of demolition and redevelopment with flats and as a method of conserving these buildings they must be welcomed.

'On the whole, conservation has moved forward in a positive way over the last twenty years and the public and politicians have become far more sensitive to conservation issues. Some twenty-five years ago, a scheme was proposed to remove all the civic buildings in Lord Street and replace them with a central area shopping redevelopment scheme. The scheme almost succeeded and if it had, Southport would look like many other towns whose heart was torn out in the '60s.

'Looking ahead, Southport should be mindful of the threat of traffic, which will continue to expand. Traffic can dictate many things, like removal of trees for safety reasons, removal of gardens for parking and narrowing of pavements to increase road widths. The challenge of the '90s is that we provide for increased traffic but do not destroy the environment we seek to keep.

'We must also carry out the tasks of refurbishing Lord Street to a high standard and if we succeed in this we will attract visitors to Southport as surely as Thomas Mawson's designs did. Visitors are the life blood of Southport and substantial investment in the future attractiveness of Southport will not be wasted,' says Mr Perry.

Although things have been looking up in the '80s, we still have to be on our guard. Conservation is still not an integral part of planning; it is regarded as something separate. Planning departments are so understaffed relative to the magnitude and pace of redevelopment today that details and aesthetics are likely to be overlooked. Periods of a more cavalier government policy towards the environment tend to deter planners from saying no when appeals to the secretary of state are likely to win or there is a risk of detering investments. There are still Philistines among us and, just as their rule was overthrown in the mid-1970s, there could be a backlash against conservation and good taste. It is evident that the man in the street supports the Prince of Wales in his views of good and bad in modern architecture and that the architect profession, from its reaction, is contemptuous of public opinion.

We cannot entirely blame architects for modern architecture. One factor is that labourers and craftsmen are better off than they were in our grandfathers' days, so labour and materials are relatively more costly. Restrictive cost limits don't give much leeway for stylish architecture. Another factor is that architects are also designing for clients. It is the clients who pay the piper and call the tune. Prestige building, which once meant monolithic classical architecture as a symbol of reliability, now means projecting a modern image to symbolise efficiency.

There is a prevailing inferiority complex about appearing old fashioned but with the unreliable reputation of much that purports to be modern and the public dislike of glass and concrete boxes, there has been a return to the more solid, handsome and ornate styles of the past. Much of the modern architecture in the developing north African countries is quite comely because it shows some deference to traditional Muslim architecture. It shows how traditional styles can be used in essentially modern buildings.

Most modern architects argue that it is not healthy to perpetuate or revive old styles and that architecture must be creative. I only wish we could evolve a new style.

If modern architecture has created nothing better, if we are incapable of evolving a new style that is more pleasing and if people prefer to be surrounded by, say, Tudor or Georgian architecture, then why not build in the old styles?

It is interesting to note that modern house building is generally traditional in style, which points to the fact that most people don't want to live in modern style buildings even if they tolerate them downtown.

It is important that the public develop an awareness and interest in architecture and that the local planning authority is better able to represent public interest with more potent power to influence the development and design of their town and to veto an unwanted development once and for all.

For those of us who live and work and do business in buildings and streets, architecture is the major element of environment. We must remind architects, planners and politicians it is our environment they are handling and see they shape it the way we like it.

Environment is a very important factor in our lives—much more than many people realise. Our environment in the first few years of our lives shapes the kind of people we are. As we grow up we become more aware of our environment and the qualities of that environment have a direct effect on our personal qualities.

When whole streets of shops, offices, flats and houses are built in off-the-shelf modern designs or prefabricated sections—plain walls, sheets of glass and cheap fabric that weathers badly—it becomes horrific; the once friendly looking streets of our towns take on the aspect of a Siberian jail. Many rebuilt towns have lost their townscapes with unrelated buildings in an urban desert carved up by motor racetracks.

Man does not live by bread alone. It is our duty to beautify this Earth and our life on it. We have a long way to go; we have wasted a lot of resources destroying beauty, the Earth and life and planning for the short-term. When we build, we should build for the long-term future, as did our forefathers who gave us the beauty and character of the Southport we know today. People who live in less comely places and towns disfigured in the 1960s and '70s want cheering up and to see some beauty in their own lifetime. We should not bide time with makeshift blocks and leave it to future generations to do it for us.

# Index

## A



## B



## C



## D



## E



## G



## H



## J



## K



## L

## W



## Y